Assuring Access in Key Strategic Regions

Toward a Long-Term Strategy

ERIC V. LARSON, DEREK EATON, PAUL ELRICK,

THEODORE KARASIK, ROBERT KLEIN, SHERRILL LINGEL,

BRIAN NICHIPORUK, ROBERT UY, JOHN ZAVADIL

Prepared for the United States Army

Approved for public release, distribution unlimited

ARROYO CENTER

The research described in this report was sponsored by the United States Army under Contract No. DASW01-01-C-0003.

Library of Congress Cataloging-in-Publication Data

Assuring Access in Key Strategic Regions : Toward a Long Term Strategy / Eric V. Larson ... [et al.].
   p. cm.
   Includes bibliographical references.
   "MG-112."
   ISBN 0-8330-3544-4 (pbk.)
   1. Deployment (Strategy) 2. United States. Army. 3. Military doctrine—United States. 4. Operational art (Military science) 5. World politics—21st century. 6. Asymmetric warfare. I. Larson, Eric V. (Eric Victor), 1957–

U163.T68 2004
355.4'773—dc22

2004000101

The RAND Corporation is a nonprofit research organization providing objective analysis and effective solutions that address the challenges facing the public and private sectors around the world. RAND's publications do not necessarily reflect the opinions of its research clients and sponsors.

RAND® is a registered trademark.

Published 2004 by the RAND Corporation
1700 Main Street, P.O. Box 2138, Santa Monica, CA 90407-2138
1200 South Hayes Street, Arlington, VA 22202-5050
201 North Craig Street, Suite 202, Pittsburgh, PA 15213-1516
RAND URL: http://www.rand.org/
To order RAND documents or to obtain additional information, contact
Distribution Services: Telephone: (310) 451-7002;
Fax: (310) 451-6915; Email: order@rand.org

Preface

This is the final report of a Fiscal Year 2002 study for the U.S. Army Deputy Chief of Staff for Operations (G-3), titled "Anti-Anti-Access: Ensuring Regional Access for Future U.S. Land Forces," which examined potential adversaries' anti-access strategies and potential U.S. counters to these strategies.

The purpose of the study was twofold. First, it aimed to support the Army's development of transformed land forces by identifying access requirements, potential anti-access threats and counters, and coalition/alliance dependencies during the 2003–2012 time period. This time frame was chosen because it is the focus of current Army planning and because it is nearly impossible to have much certainty about potential adversary capabilities beyond that period. Second, it considers operational and technical means for overcoming anti-access threats. This report summarizes the main findings of the study; some unpublished research about the study has also been done, including the following titles:

- "Anti-Access in a Baltic Scenario," 2003;
- "Anti-Access in a SWA Scenario," 2003;
- "Anti-Access in a PRC-Taiwan Scenario," 2003; and
- "Anti-Access Strategies: A Quantitative Analysis of Military Methods for Preventing, Delaying, and Degrading U.S. Force Buildups," 2003.

The project was sponsored by the Office of the Deputy Chief of Staff G-3 (Operations and Plans), U.S. Army. The project was conducted in the Strategy, Doctrine, and Resources Program of the RAND Arroyo Center. The Arroyo Center is a federally funded research and development center sponsored by the U.S. Army.

For more information on RAND Arroyo Center, contact the Director of Operations (telephone 310-393-0411, extension 6419; FAX 310-451-6952; e-mail Marcy_Agmon@rand.org), or visit Arroyo's web site at http://www.rand.org/ard/.

Contents

CHAPTER SEVEN

What the Games Revealed About Anti-Access Threats

CHAPTER EIGHT

Toward a Strategy for Assuring Access

Figures and Tables

Summary

Since the end of the Cold War, agreement within the defense community that the United States must be able to project power abroad quickly and effectively has been increasing. From the 1990 Base Force's emphasis on forward presence and crisis response to the 1997 Quadrennial Defense Review's strategic tenets of "shape and respond," U.S. defense planning has envisioned the reinforcement of in-theater forces.[1] The most recent (September 2001) Quadrennial Defense Review (QDR) gave increased emphasis to deployability, operations in anti-access environments, and protecting bases of operation at home and abroad.[2]

Even as the Army transforms its forces to be more deployable, however, U.S. adversaries continue to develop asymmetric strategies and means, among which we would include efforts to complicate U.S. access to a theater of operation—adversary anti-access strategies. Adversary anti-access strategies can be defined in a very broad way; in our conception, these are strategies

---

[1] Following publication of the 1997 QDR, the December 1997 report of the National Defense Panel identified access issues as an area of key concern. See National Defense Panel, *Transforming Defense: National Security in the 21st Century*, Washington, D.C., December 1997.

[2] The 2001 QDR states that "projecting and sustaining U.S. forces in distant anti-access or area-denial environments and defeating anti-access and area-denial threats" is one of the Department of Defense's (DoD's) six operational goals driving transformation of the force.

- "whose aim is to deter, prevent, degrade, disrupt, delay, or otherwise complicate the mobilization, deployment, entry, and buildup of U.S. forces for military operations in a theater;
- "that can be executed during peacetime, in crisis, and in conflict and that can involve strategic, operational, and/or tactical methods (strategic methods can include military, diplomatic, political, economic, psychological, and other measures whose effects transform the nature of the conflict; operational methods can include actions that force the United States to operate from a greater than preferred range; and tactical methods can include conventional and unconventional capabilities that can hinder deployment and onward movement);
- "that may involve actions against continental U.S. (CONUS), en-route, or in-theater targets;
- "that may be integrated with broader national strategies to include actions that are executed during peacetime, crisis, and conflict; and
- "that may involve actions taken either by an adversary or by its proxies.

In the context of the Army's ongoing transformation efforts, it is difficult in the abstract to determine the level of threat posed by the growing repertoire of anti-access tools that potential adversaries may have available in the near- and longer-term future. This report aims to make the anti-access threat more tangible by assessing the efficacy of anti-access strategies—and U.S. and coalition counters—in a small but diverse set of conflict scenarios.

Defining the Access Game

In exploring these scenarios, the study team made efforts to examine how the character of the competition between the United States and a potential adversary might evolve in peacetime, crisis, and war and what this might imply for U.S. strategy and force development. This work gave rise to a construct we called "the access game," in which the United States and a potential regional adversary would, through trial and error, seek to shape the future access outlook for the United States.

The access game envisions that during peacetime the adversary will seek to deter both U.S. involvement in the region and regional cooperation with the United States. It also foresees adversary efforts to shape the U.S. access environment by coercing U.S. regional partners and allies to withhold access. As the situation moves from peacetime to crisis and war, the adversary may use a variety of political, economic, and military means to, first, prevent the United States from gaining access and, failing that, to delay or degrade the buildup and onward movement of U.S. forces.

Meanwhile, in peacetime, the United States will seek to assure partners and allies in handling internal and external threats to their security while deterring the adversary, and preempting and countering its peacetime maneuvering to restrict or otherwise shape the U.S. access outlook. As the situation moves to crisis and war, the U.S. aim will shift to mitigating or overcoming adversary actions to prevent, delay, or degrade the buildup of U.S. forces. For each of the scenarios the study team examined in seminar gaming, we considered the nature of the peacetime, crisis, and wartime actions that might be taken by the United States and its putative adversary and what key challenges and opportunities might present themselves.

Findings

Findings from Scenario Gaming

Our consideration of the access game in the context of the scenarios led us to conclude that, while adversary anti-access strategies are not the only strategies available and others, such as strategies of annihilation and attrition, also need to be considered, we believe that the anti-access threat is a serious and growing one. To reduce U.S. vulnerability to adversary anti-access strategies, the Army and DoD should pursue a range of options that would improve the access-enhancing characteristics of U.S. forces. These options include

- further diversifying the U.S. portfolio of prospective bases and mobility capabilities while reducing their requirements for mature infrastructure;
- improving the self-deployability of some forces to underwrite new deployment concepts and warfighting concepts; and
- ensuring capabilities for rapidly assaulting, seizing, and improving bases to make them suitable for the conduct of operations.

The conflict scenarios used in the study were designed with the aim of illuminating anti-access strategies and threats in peacetime, crisis, and war in four geographic areas of responsibility—European, Pacific, Central, and Southern Command. The scenarios featured adversaries at the high end of the capability scale in each region—i.e., those who would be expected to have recourse to the most potent and diverse portfolio of anti-access strategies and capabilities. Occasionally, the scenarios sacrificed detail in areas that seemed less relevant to access issues to better illuminate the character of potential access challenges.

We explored anti-access in a Southwest Asia scenario in which Iraq was assumed to be months away from acquiring a nuclear weapon. We also examined an East Asia scenario in which the People's Republic of China sought to resolve the issue of Taiwan's status through military means. We also analyzed a European scenario in which Russia undertook an attack on the Baltic states under the guise of protecting Russian minorities. Finally, we considered in somewhat less detail a range of less-than-war operations in Central and South America.

While our assessments of these scenarios led to a reasonably sanguine view of U.S. ability to prevail in each, a number of threats were cause for concern. These will be discussed next.

Adversary Actions Taken for Strategic Political or Psychological Impact Are Likely to Prove Most Successful. Our principal findings from the scenario analyses were as follows:

- Because their weapon systems are likely to lack range, accuracy, and payload during the 2003–2012 period we examined, adversaries are likely to have more incentives to use anti-access military capabilities against regional leadership, population, and high-profile soft military targets rather than attempting to destroy a whole set of bases or other anti-access targets. Moreover, nonmilitary means (cooptation, coercion, subversion, information operations, and psychological operations) may in fact prove to be more effective than military means in achieving anti-access objectives.

- For the same reason, attacks on bases and other infrastructure are more likely to prove successful for their psychological value—raising the costs of a military action in the hope of getting policymakers to reconsider—than the military significance of what they can reliably destroy.

- Control of chokepoints, while likely to be short-lived, can have important operational impacts on the role of land forces and on campaign outcomes and measures of effectiveness.

- Most adversaries presently lack strategic reach except through special operations forces or terrorist proxies and therefore appear to have limited opportunities to conduct anti-access attacks outside of their immediate theater of operation. Nevertheless, important "wild cards" exist, such as longer-range ballistic missiles with nuclear warheads, that should not be entirely ruled out.

- Technological trends are such that anti-access capabilities could substantially improve beyond the 2012 horizon we examined. The United States needs to anticipate these trends and begin to take measures now that would prevent potential adversaries from achieving any new, decisive anti-access capabilities. The proliferation of nuclear weapons, highly accurate ballistic and cruise missiles, or advanced SAMs would be particularly worrisome.

Our analysis of these scenarios suggested that greater concern is warranted for actions that might be taken for strategic political or psychological impact than for those that are strictly military in nature. In particular, adversaries seemed to have a wide variety of nonmilitary carrots and sticks that they might employ to complicate or restrict the U.S. access outlook in a region, and in many ways these were more worrisome than the military methods. In several of the scenarios, the study team saw great potential for psychological operations and propaganda as a tool for imposing costs on regional partners and allies for their cooperation with the United States. This was especially acute in the Southwest Asia scenario, where Iraq cynically sought to link its own situation to the Palestinian issue in the minds of regional Arab and Muslim populations and to erode support for the United States by highlighting its continued support for Israel. It also played in the Baltics scenario, where Russia's claims that it was acting defensively against an expanding NATO found fertile soil among German Greens and peace groups.

The Threats Likely to Be Faced by U.S. Land Forces Through 2012 Should Be Relatively Manageable, but Could Cause Delays. Numerous instances occurred in which adversaries' military anti-access capabilities had the operational consequence of forcing the United States to operate, at least initially, from greater distance. However, in none of these games could adversaries actually deny the United States access, or sufficiently delay or degrade access to prevent U.S. forces from successfully accomplishing their missions. Thus, the scenario gaming generally seemed to suggest that nonnuclear military anti-access threats should be pretty manageable out to 2012, even as the study team broadly recognized that these threats could become far more potent after 2012. Nuclear threats remained an important wild card in our scenario gaming in the sense that we believed that in most cases use of nuclear weapons would be deterred, but actual use could either destroy needed bases or potentially deter policymakers from continuing with a military operation.

As just described, the scenario gaming had suggested a reasonably sanguine view of the anti-access problem. Accordingly, the study team analyzed another case in which most would expect, a priori, that anti-access strategies should have some sort of impact on campaign outcomes—Iranian closure of the Strait of Hormuz, the anti-access threat par excellence.

Analysis of the Iran scenario in fact provided compelling evidence that under some conditions—in this case, where a committed adversary was in the geographically advantageous position of controlling a key chokepoint—anti-access strategies can have substantial impacts. More specifically, this modeling suggested that as the delays in the arrival of land forces increased as a result of closure of the strait, campaign outcomes deteriorated, even to the point where strategically important facilities might be lost. Thus, the campaign modeling provided an existence proof for the proposition that the success of campaigns could, under some limiting conditions, pivot on the question of timely access. The modeling also showed that several weeks with the loss of the strait could mean that U.S. land forces might play only a very limited role in blunting the offensive.

The U.S. Army and the Joint Community Need to Consider a Wider Range of Anti-Access Scenarios. Taken together, the analysis of these conflict scenarios suggested that the anti-access threat is a heterogeneous one that varies by adversary, the adversary's political effectiveness in regional political and security affairs, military capability levels, geography, and a number of other factors. It also suggests that the overall potency of the *military* anti-access threat may hinge on the geographic circumstance of the adversary, especially its proximity to and ability to threaten or control chokepoints, sea lines of communication, and corridors for ingressing aircraft. Absent a favorable combination of such circumstances, the impact of adversaries' anti-access strategies generally would be expected to be relatively modest.

This differentiated view of the anti-access threat suggests to us that the Army and joint community need to consider the anti-access issue in greater detail in the context of a wide range of scenarios. Additional campaign modeling and analysis of the anti-access options available to adversaries are needed, both for the standard planning scenarios used for force planning and for regional commanders' contingency and operational plans. As in so many cases of analysis, the details really do matter.

Toward an Access Strategy

These results, coupled with the earlier efforts on the access game begun in the early phases of the study, suggested a general Army and joint strategy for assuring access, with peacetime, crisis, and wartime elements.

In this strategy, during peacetime, the United States should undertake activities that can reassure partners and allies and deter adversaries. Execution of the theater security cooperation plan and Army international activities (AIA), including exercises, military training, military-to-military contacts, and other activities can further this. So too can the sale of systems that can, as in the case of layered theater air and missile defenses, reduce the threat of coercion in crisis and war or increase the interoperability of U.S. and friendly forces in specific areas that may redound favorably on forced entry and force protection.

But the United States also should develop new options that can expand the portfolio of potential bases and infrastructure that might be used in a military operation. A range of complementary means is available to accomplish this.

First, access options can be improved by increasing the number of possible bases and other infrastructure that might be available. This can be accomplished in part through negotiations aimed at providing access to additional bases or to allow prepositioning. In some cases, partners and allies might build new facilities or improve existing ones, with many possible cost-sharing arrangements and other means of giving incentives for such efforts. Finally, investment in sea-based prepositioning or sea bases might improve the access outlook.

Second, the flexibility of mobility might be improved so that mobility assets simply are capable of operating in less developed environments. To the extent that the mobility force's current reliance on mature infrastructure can be reduced and a "go anywhere" mobility force can be created, the access outlook will greatly improve. For example, a mix of shallow-draft sealift, lighterage, and organic docking capabilities could reduce the reliance of the sealift force on deep-water ports and wide berths. Development of a C-17/C-130 transshipment concept of operations might similarly improve the access outlook.

Third, the deployability of forces might be improved to make them more expeditionary, such that their basing, sustainment, and lift requirements can be reduced. By improving the deployability of air and theater missile defenses, for example, it will be easier to assure partners and allies who are facing ballistic missile threats and to move missile defenses in more quickly. By improving the deployability of long-range fires—and developing concepts of operation for their use as an alternative to ground maneuver forces—land forces might be able to play an earlier and more important role in halting an attacking enemy's advance. The cost-effectiveness of such capabilities would need to be compared with sea-based and aviation alternatives. Finally, improving the self-deployability of some forces, such as attack helicopters, may facilitate both deployment directly into the combat zone and dispersed operations and thereby improve their access-enhancing characteristics.

Fourth, Detection, Warning, and Force Protection Measures at Key Bases Can Be Improved. By improving the ability to detect and warn of conventional and unconventional attacks and improving force protection and other defensive measures, the impacts of many attacks might be mitigated.

In crisis and war, the United States will need to deploy military forces and defend both deploying forces and the infrastructure they need. In many cases, the leadership and populations of the host nations also will need to be defended. In some cases, U.S. forces may need to improve, seize, or build access: *improving* existing inadequate infrastructure, forcibly *seizing* the needed infrastructure, or *building* new infrastructure. Finally, to ensure continued access, U.S. forces will need to protect forces and bases of operation.

Thus, any long-term access strategy for the Army and DoD will involve placing bets across a wide range of activities, while remaining alert to, and adapting to, the unexpected.

Acknowledgments

The authors wish to acknowledge LTC Steven Lanza of DAMO-SSP, who served as project monitor during most of the project. The report also benefited from comments on an earlier briefing from DAMO-SSP, Eric Kramer, and the J-8's Dominant Maneuver Task Force. We also thank Dave Kassing and Lauri Zeman, who served as Program Directors for Arroyo's Strategy, Doctrine, and Resources Program during the project, and Tom Szayna, Assistant Program Director, for his exceedingly useful comments on earlier outputs of the study. We also would like to acknowledge the assistance of Paul Elrick, a visiting researcher from the Defence Science and Technology Laboratory (Dstl), a research organization that supports the British Ministry of Defence. Within RAND, we also express our gratitude to Amy Atchison, Richard Bancroft, Barbara Neff, Leroy Reyes, and Roberta Shanman of RAND's library; Laurie Rennie, for organizing our many meetings and exercises; and Barbara Genovese, Rebeca Bower, and Terri Perkins, for their help in assembling data and preparing manuscripts. We also thank our two reviewers, Glenn Buchan of RAND and Chip Franck of the Naval Postgraduate School, for their thoughtful comments and suggestions on an earlier draft of this report. Finally, we thank Chris Bowie, formerly of the Northrop Grumman Corporation, for sharing his anti-access study with us.

Glossary

AB	Air Base
AMC	Air Mobility Command
APOD	Aerial Point of Debarkation
APOE	Aerial Port of Embarkation
APS	Active Protection System
ARCENT	(U.S.) Army Forces Central Command
ARPAC	(U.S.) Army Forces Pacific Command
ARSOUTH	(U.S.) Army Forces Southern Command
ASAT	Antisatellite
ASW	Antisubmarine Warfare
ATACMS	Army Tactical Missile System
AWACS	Airborne Warning and Control System
BCT	Brigade Combat Team
C2	Command and Control
CBRNE	Chemical, Biological, Radiological, Nuclear, or High Explosive
CENTCOM	(U.S.) Central Command
CEP	Circular Error Probable
CONUS	Continental United States
EMP	Electromagnetic Pulse

ERA   Explosive Reactive Armor

EUCOM   (U.S.) European Command

EW   Electronic Warfare

FARC   Revolutionary Armed Forces of Colombia

GCC   Gulf Cooperation Council

IADS   Integrated Air Defense System

ICBM   Intercontinental Ballistic Missile

IED   Improvised Explosive Device

IISS   International Institute for Strategic Studies

IND   Improvised Nuclear Device

IO   Information Operations

IRBM   Intermediate-Range Ballistic Missile

ISR   Intelligence, Surveillance, and Reconnaissance

JLOTS   Joint Logistics over the Shore

JSTARS   Joint Surveillance and Target Attack Radar
                        System

LACM   Land-Attack Cruise Missile

LMSR   Large, Medium-Speed, Roll-On/Roll-Off
                        (ships)

LOC   Line of Communications

MCM   Mine Countermeasures

MEF   Marine Expeditionary Force

MEU   Marine Expeditionary Unit

MHE   Material-Handling Equipment

MLRS   Multiple-Launch Rocket System

MOD   Ministry of Defence (U.K.)

MOG   Maximum on Ground (aircraft)

NATO   North Atlantic Treaty Organization

NBC	Nuclear, Biological, and Chemical
NEO	Noncombatant Evacuation Operation
NTA	Nontraditional Agents
NV	Night Vision
PACOM	(U.S.) Pacific Command
PLA	People's Liberation Army (China)
PLAAF	People's Liberation Army Air Force (China)
PRC	People's Republic of China
QDR	Quadrennial Defense Review
R&D	Research and Development
RF	Radio Frequency
RO/RO	Roll-On/Roll-Off
RPG	Rocket-Propelled Grenade
SAM	Surface-to-Air Missile
SBCT	Stryker Brigade Combat Team
SEAD	Suppression of Enemy Air Defenses
SLOC	Sea Line of Communication
SOF	Special Operations Forces
SOUTHCOM	(U.S.) Southern Command
SPOD	Sea-Based Point of Debarkation
SPOD	Seaport of Debarkation
SPOE	Seaport of Embarkation
SRBM	Short-Range Ballistic Missile
SSK	Diesel Submarine with ASW
SWA	Southwest Asia
TBM	Theater Ballistic Missile
TEL	Transporter-Erector-Launcher
THAAD	Theater High-Altitude Area Defense

TMD	Theater Missile Defense
TSV	Theater Support Vessel
UAE	United Arab Emirates
UAV	Unmanned Aerial Vehicle
UCAV	Unmanned Combat Air Vehicle
USAF	U.S. Air Force
USAREUR	U.S. Army European Command
USMC	U.S. Marine Corp
WMD	Weapon(s) of Mass Destruction

CHAPTER ONE

Introduction

With the end of the Cold War, the United States entered an era in which the nation is politically, economically, and militarily without peer. The same era has also seen increasing agreement that the Army must be able to project power abroad quickly and effectively.

The 1989–1990 major defense review that resulted in the Base Force fashioned a new post–Cold War posture. This posture would be characterized less by the Cold War–era principles of containment and forward defense underwritten by permanently stationed forces than by the new post–Cold War era principles of forward presence and crisis response.[1] The implication of this change in posture was profound: the United States would rely less on permanently stationed forward-deployed forces and more on rotational deployments of U.S.-based forces to regions of strategic significance and on power projection from the United States for crisis response.

The outcome of the 1991 Persian Gulf War gave potential future adversaries every reason to believe that, unless the United States could be deterred or prevented from projecting forces into a theater of operation, its quantitative preponderance and qualitative advantages in advanced military capabilities inevitably would lead to a U.S. victory.

---

[1] For a review of the 1989–1990 Base Force, the 1993 Bottom-Up Review, and the 1997 Quadrennial Defense Review, see Eric V. Larson, David T. Orletsky, and Kristin Leuschner, *Defense Planning in a Decade of Change*, Santa Monica, Calif.: RAND Corporation, MR-1387-AF, 2001.

With potential adversaries thus unable to challenge the United States directly with symmetric military capabilities, concern grew in the defense establishment that nations that could not match the United States in conventional military capabilities would look for other ways to counter U.S. forces and offset its military advantages. While the putative list of so-called "asymmetric" strategies and means is theoretically vast, the efficacy of these strategies and means will in practice be greatly constrained by the actual suitability and effectiveness of a potential adversary's anti-access capabilities, geographic and terrain features, regional dynamics, and constraints that are imposed on operations.

The September 2001 Quadrennial Defense Review (QDR) gave increased emphasis to deployability, operations in anti-access environments, and protecting bases of operation. Even as the Army transforms its forces to become, among other things, more deployable, U.S. adversaries continue to develop asymmetric strategies and means,[2] including efforts to complicate, deny, or delay U.S. access to a theater of operation. For most of the duration of our study, no broad analytic examinations of anti-access threats to land forces in the emerging threat environment existed,[3] especially ones related to land forces. Most of those that emerged over the course of the study dealt with specific aspects of the anti-access challenge as they related to naval or air forces, for example, or to the potential impacts on interdiction capabilities in a combined-arms campaign.[4] Our study

---

[2] For a *tour d'horizon* of asymmetric strategies, see Bruce W. Bennett, Christopher P. Twomey, and Gregory F. Treverton, *What Are Asymmetric Strategies?* Santa Monica, Calif.: RAND Corporation, DB-246-OSD, 1999. Literature also offers many potential adversary asymmetric strategies: targeting Achilles' unprotected heel, David felling the giant Goliath with a well-placed precision-guided stone, and the Lilliputians tying Gulliver down with hundreds of threads.

[3] During our study, the Office of Net Assessment in the Office of the Secretary of Defense completed a classified study on the broader question of anti-access threats, however.

[4] Five relatively recent studies or papers on the anti-access issue are Owen R. Coté, Jr., *Assuring Access and Projecting Power: The Navy in the New Security Environment*, Cambridge, Mass.: MIT Security Studies Program, 2000, and Arthur H. Barber III and Delwyn L. Gilmore, "Maritime Access: Do Defenders Hold All the Cards?" *Defense Horizons*, Washington, D.C.: Center for National Security Policy, National Defense University, October 2001,

accordingly took a "wide aperture" view of anti-access challenges in the large, while accenting their implications for land forces.

Many elements of the U.S. force projection chain are potentially vulnerable to anti-access efforts. To attain access, the Army relies on a projection platform that includes U.S. bases, fort-to-port movements, aerial ports of embarkation (APOEs) and seaports of embarkation (SPOEs), strategic mobility assets, land- and sea-based prepositioning, transit routes, en-route bases, in-theater aerial ports of debarkation (APODs) and seaports of debarkation (SPODs), and onward movement within the theater. Moreover, the global network of enroute and in-theater bases—many of which are on foreign soil—is potentially vulnerable to adversary coercive efforts to persuade U.S. partners to deny access to U.S. forces. The attacks of September 11, 2001, provide a chilling reminder that deploying forces—along with civilians—could face attacks in the continental United States (CONUS).

Anti-access means can include a range of political, military, and other actions to coerce the United States and its partners and allies or to place at risk deploying forces, their bases, and needed infrastructure. Such means include threatened or actual use of weapons of mass destruction (WMD), cruise and ballistic missiles, attack submarines, sea mines, special operations and conventional terrorism, information warfare (IW), and other techniques, each of which offers the prospects of growing both in terms of sophistication and availability.

In the context of the Army's ongoing transformation efforts, it is difficult in the abstract to determine the level of threat posed by the growing repertoire of anti-access tools that potential adversaries might have in the near- and longer-term future. This report aims to make the anti-access threat more tangible by presenting the results of an

---

which accent anti-access issues that are of principal concern to the Navy; Christopher J. Bowie, *The Anti-Access Threat and Theater Air Bases*, Washington, D.C.: Center for Strategic and Budgetary Assessments, 2002; David Shlapak et al., *A Global Access Strategy for the U.S. Air Force*, Santa Monica, Calif.: RAND Corporation, MR-1216-AF, 2002, and Paul K. Davis, Jimmie McEver, and Barry Wilson, *Measuring Interdiction Capabilities in the Presence of Anti-Access Strategies: Exploratory Analysis to Inform Adaptive Strategy for the Persian Gulf*, Santa Monica, Calif.: RAND Corporation, MR-1471-AF, 2002, each of which accents access and anti-access issues most relevant to the Air Force.

assessment of the efficacy of anti-access strategies—and U.S. and coalition counters—in a number of specific conflict scenarios.

Before proceeding, it is important to state our belief that anti-access strategies are not the only—nor necessarily even the best—strategies that may be available to future U.S. adversaries. Other strategies may under many conditions be superior to—or important complements of—anti-access strategies.[5] Thus, this report should be read in light of its intended purpose—an effort to illuminate the issues associated with adversary anti-access strategies and capabilities, and to highlight the characteristics of anti-access threats and strategies that differentiate them from other threats and strategies.

Organization of This Report

This report is organized as follows:

- Chapter Two provides background on the anti-access problem and describes the approach used by the study team.
- Chapters Three through Six provide the results of the scenario gaming we used as the principal means to explore anti-access threats and counters and to identify actions that regional commanders can take to better manage evolving anti-access threats in their regions.
- Chapter Seven pulls the various scenarios together to explain what the scenario gaming reveals about anti-access threats.
- Chapter Eight describes a long-term strategy for addressing future anti-access challenges, including actions that the Department of the Army, Joint Staff, and Department of Defense

---

[5] For example, strategies of annihilation and attrition were considered by classical military theorists as opposite poles on a continuum of military strategies. See Peter Paret, *Makers of Modern Strategy: From Machiavelli to the Nuclear Age*, Oxford, UK: Clarendon Press, 1990, p. 57. The military theoretician Hans Delbrück conceived of two forms of warfare, one that embraced a strategy of annihilation, whose aim was the decisive battle, and a strategy of exhaustion, which consisted of battle and maneuver (Paret, 1990, pp. 341–344).

(DoD) might consider to better organize, train, and equip land forces to meet anti-access challenges.

- Chapter Nine provides some concluding thoughts, particularly with regard to the study's implications for intelligence needs.[6]

---

[6] An appendix, published separately (for official use only), identifies preferred en-route and in-theater basing for each region, as well as alternatives that should be explored to better hedge against the potential success of adversary anti-access strategies in each region.

CHAPTER TWO

Analytic Approach

The study relied upon a three-pronged approach. The first was to develop conceptual building blocks that would assist the study team in understanding the interplay between potential anti-access threats and counters in general terms. The second was to compile forecasts of future military capabilities and assess quantitatively the military utility of various types of weapons. The third was to develop a series of seminar-style games in which the team could explore the interplay of anti-access strategies and counterstrategies in the context of concrete scenarios and forecasts of adversary and U.S. capabilities. Each will be described.

Some Conceptual Building Blocks

The first task was to develop the conceptual building blocks that could provide a common framework for assessing future adversary anti-access capabilities and counters. In all, four were developed: a definition of adversary anti-access strategies, a characterization of what came to be called "the access game," a stylized representation of the deployment process, and a characterization of potential vulnerabilities in the deployment process.

A Definition for Anti-Access Strategies

We defined adversary anti-access strategies in a very broad way, to ensure that we didn't artificially impose constraints on the analysis that might lead us to miss important features of the anti-access problem. In our conception, adversary anti-access strategies are strategies

- whose aim is to deter, prevent, degrade, disrupt, delay, or otherwise complicate the mobilization, deployment, entry, and buildup of U.S. forces for military operations in a theater;
- that can be executed during peacetime, in crisis, and in conflict;
- that can involve strategic, operational, and tactical methods. Strategic methods can include military, diplomatic, political, economic, and psychological measures whose effects transform the nature of the conflict; operational methods can include actions that force the United States to operate from a greater than preferred range; and tactical methods can include conventional and unconventional capabilities that can be used locally to hinder deployment and onward movement;
- that may involve actions against CONUS, en-route, or in-theater targets;
- that may be integrated with broader national strategies to include actions executed during peacetime, crisis, and conflict; and
- that may involve actions taken either by an adversary or by his proxies.[1]

The Access Game

Our view was that while the specific strategies, ways, and means might vary greatly from situation to situation, in most cases adversary anti-access strategies and U.S. counters would be embedded in a larger game that would be played out in peacetime, during crisis, and in war. We called this process "the access game" (see Figure 2.1).

---

[1] Bowie (2002, p. 1) also uses a fairly broad definition of anti-access threats, suggesting they are "the complex mix of political, geographic, and military factors that could prevent or delay U.S. forces from deploying to a combat theater."

Figure 2.1
Overview of the Access Game

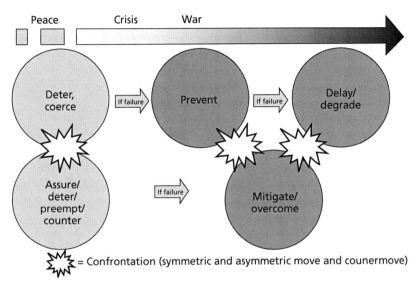

RAND MG112-2.1

As suggested by the figure, during peacetime a potential adversary (top half of figure) generally will seek, first, to influence—or coerce—U.S. partners and allies in the region in ways that will reduce the likelihood that they might provide the sorts of access that the United States might need in a crisis or conflict.[2] In the transition from peacetime to crisis, the adversary probably would continue to influence and coerce, as well as take a range of other actions to try to deter the United States from acting on behalf of a regional friend or ally.

At the same time, the United States (bottom half of figure) will be undertaking a range of peacetime and crisis actions to better

---

[2] One can conceive of noncoercive influence as using available diplomatic, economic, and other tools to increase areas of policy agreement and cooperation such that the net effect is a closer alignment of interests between the adversary and U.S. regional partners and allies and an erosion in their basis for security cooperation with the United States. Coercion also could involve a mix of "carrots" and "sticks." See Alexander L. George and William E. Simons, *The Limits of Coercive Diplomacy*, second edition, Boulder, Colo.: Westview Press, 1994.

ensure access. These actions include assuring regional partners and allies of U.S. ability to make a decisive contribution to their security in the event of crisis or conflict—as well as assuring them of the credibility of its security commitments—and preempting or countering the adversary's efforts to restrict future U.S. access to the region.

In the transitions to crisis and war, the adversary will supplement its earlier efforts with more-direct efforts to prevent U.S. access or, failing that objective, delay or degrade U.S. access. Meanwhile, the United States will attempt to mitigate or overcome the adversary's efforts.

As shown in Figures 2.2 and 2.3, both the adversary and the United States can be conceived of as having strategies that exhibit "trial and error" and a "graceful failure mode" that engender experimentation in ascertaining the most effective means of achieving objectives, with successive fallback positions should favored means prove disappointing.

As shown in Figure 2.2, the adversary's "best" option is to *deter* U.S. action in the first instance, or *coerce* or otherwise *influence* others to deny access to the United States, because deterrence and coercion might be achieved through threats alone and without actual recourse to the use of force. Failing deterrence and coercion, the adversary's "second-best" option is to try to *prevent* U.S. access, which may lead to attacks on regional actors or U.S. facilities and forces. If the adversary is unable to prevent U.S. access, its "third-best" option is to take actions to *delay* or *degrade* the buildup of U.S. forces in the hope that it can achieve its initial objectives (e.g., seizing a strategic prize, such as a capital or oilfields), or it may dramatically increase the risks to the execution of operational plans by degrading or delaying U.S. forces sufficiently to threaten mission accomplishment or by increasing the likely costs to friendly forces of favored courses of action, so as to deter specific operational actions.

By comparison, "best" strategy for U.S. Forces (see Figure 2.3) is to try to *assure* partners and *deter* adversaries, and to *anticipate* and

Figure 2.2
The Adversary's Adaptive Strategy for the Access Game

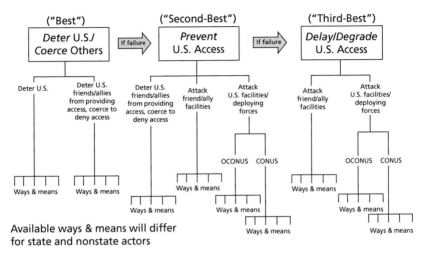

Available ways & means will differ
for state and nonstate actors

RAND *MG112-2.2*

Figure 2.3
U.S. Adaptive Strategy for the Access Game

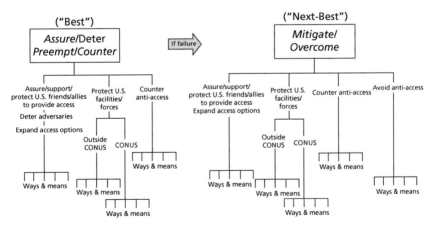

RAND *MG112-2.3*

preempt adversary actions that may result in a loss of access, in part by expanding the available access options.

Its "next best" strategy is to try to mitigate or overcome the effects of an adversary's anti-access efforts through a variety of military and nonmilitary means. In the longer term, of course, both the United States and its adversary can take actions to alter the access outlook. Both can undertake diplomatic and other initiatives to influence the affinities of other regional actors and change perceptions of the likely regional correlation of forces in the event of crisis or conflict. Both can develop or otherwise acquire new capabilities that may improve their positions in some future anti-access game, with the adversary adding capabilities that will better deter, prevent, delay, or degrade friendly forces, and the United States adding capabilities to overcome or render moot the adversary's new anti-access capabilities. U.S. forces also can hedge by increasing the range of basing and infrastructure options for any given contingency, by developing entirely new mobility concepts that are less reliant on mature air bases or seaports or by enhancing base seizure, improvement, and construction capabilities.

A Stylized Representation of a Deployment

To provide a consistent basis for evaluating the potential efficacy of adversary anti-access strategies and U.S. counters across conflict scenarios, we appropriated a stylized representation of a deployment that identified—for the U.S. homeland, the en-route leg of the deployment, and the theater of concern—bases and other installations as nodes and movements as arcs (see Figure 2.4).[3]

As shown, the figure provides a schematic that includes CONUS-based fort-to-port movements, strategic movements from

---

[3] Based on a stylized representation in Zbigniew Majchrzak, *Army Force Projection*, Fort Eustis, Va.: U.S. Army Transportation School, Deployment Process Modernization Office, 1999, p. 16, which in turn is based on an illustration in Department of the Army, Headquarters, *Movement Control*, Army Field Manual (FM) 55-10, February 9, 1999, Chapter One, pp. 1–4.

Figure 2.4
A Stylized Representation of a Deployment

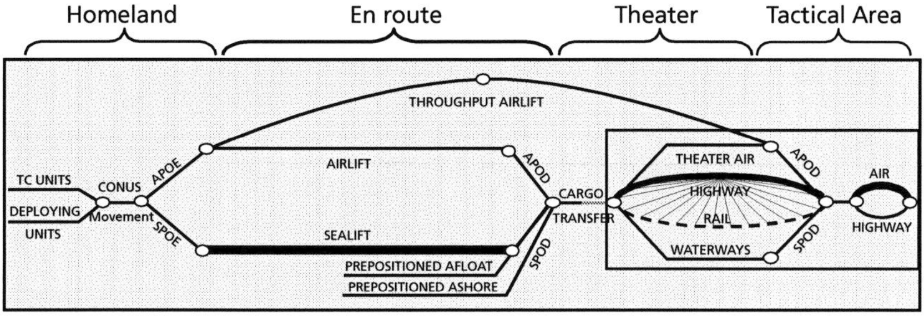

APOEs and SPOEs to APODs and SPODs, and onward movement toward the tactical area.

Our assumption was that, in theory at least, an adversary could direct attacks or other actions against any of the nodes or arcs in this figure. As a practical matter, an adversary would be expected to be limited not only by actual capabilities for undertaking actions in the United States, en route, and in theater but also by its risk orientation and willingness to take actions that might result in adverse consequences, for example, initiating a substantial—and undesirable—escalation of the situation. These issues of capabilities, intentions, risk orientation, and attitude toward escalation were among those explored in our seminar gaming.

Characterization of Potential Anti-Access Vulnerabilities

We then identified a wide range of potential vulnerabilities that an adversary might attempt to exploit to deter or otherwise influence U.S. decisionmaking on whether to undertake a military response or to disrupt the mobilization and deployment of U.S. combat forces. This work resulted in a list of potential deployment-related targets that might be attacked by an adversary.[4]

---

[4] In all, the team identified more than 50 potential sources of vulnerability associated with forts, fort-to-port movements, APOEs and SPOEs, air and sea movements, en-route bases, APODs and SPODs, and onward movement.

Quantitative Analysis of Military Utility

A second thrust of the analysis was to try to understand the military utility of potential threat systems against current and potential anti-access targets. We compiled data on trends in threat systems and identified preferred systems for attacking various types of targets.[5]

To identify preferred anti-access means, we began with our list of potential CONUS, en-route, and in-theater anti-access vulnerabilities and classified potential anti-access targets into six classes based on their size and hardness (Table 2.1).[6]

Table 2.1
Classification of Anti-Access Targets

	Small Area	Large Area
Very Soft	Aircraft Loading/Fueling Equipment Motor Pool Personnel/Vehicles	
Soft	Barracks Bridges Maintenance Shops Operations Buildings Pipelines/Pumping Equipment Rolling Stock Runways/Aprons Satellite Communications Terminals/Radrel Antennas Ships/Docks/Berths	Air Bases Bases Cities Container Terminals Large Aprons Oil Refineries Ports Power Plants Rail Yards
Hard	Aircraft Shelters Ammo Storage Armored Vehicles Cable Vaults Bunkers/Tunnels	

NOTE: Criterion for "large area" is 100,000 square meters.

---

[5] The detailed analysis is in an annotated briefing available to authorized government personnel but not available to the general public.

[6] This effort emphasized air and land weapon systems. We considered the potential effectiveness of naval and other systems in the context of our specific scenarios. We also explicitly considered salvo requirements, estimating the number of attacking weapons that would be needed to provide a high assurance of a kill.

Using an analysis of range, accuracy, weapon effects, and other factors, we then identified what might be considered preferred means for attacking each class of target—those means that could provide a reasonably high level of assurance of a target kill (Table 2.2).[1]

Seminar-Style Gaming

As described above, we used seminar-style multiscenario gaming as our principal means for assessing regional anti-access threats and counters. Our choice of gaming was the consequence both of several shared beliefs and resource constraints.

First, we believed that there was a strong potential that future anti-access threats and counters would be highly conditional on

Table 2.2
Preferred Means of Attacking Anti-Access Target Classes

	Small Area	Large Area
Very Soft	***Submunitions*** **Most Other Listed Means**	
Soft	***Guided Munitions (Including Cruise Missiles)*** ***Infantry Weapons*** **Attack Helicopters** **Artillery Rockets** **Artillery** **Aircraft Dumb Bombs** Mortars	***CBRNE*** **SOF/Terrorism** Mortars Theater Ballistic Missiles Air-Delivered Mines
Hard	***Guided Munitions (Including Cruise Missiles)*** ***Penetrating Munitions*** **SOF/Terrorism** **Infantry Weapons**	***Preferred*** **Viable Means** Harassment Only

NOTE: Criterion for "large area" is 100,000 square meters.
In the table, the most effective ("preferred") means of attack are in bold italic, means of attack that are viable but not preferred are in bold, and means that are relatively ineffective, but still might be used for harassment purposes, are in plain text. "CBRNE" means chemical, biological, radiological, nuclear, or high-explosive weapons.

regional geography, political dynamics, and other factors unique to each specific conflict situation and that we accordingly needed to examine a range of cases that would, in some sense, span the "scenario space." This dictated a multiscenario approach. Second, we believed that the pace of change in military technologies meant that historically based analyses would be a poor guide for the future. This dictated a choice of scenario gaming over historical analysis. Third, the rather ambitious research goals and the costs of a simulation modeling-based analysis resource also helped rule out a modeling approach to the problem for the simple reason that the anti-access challenge was so dominated by contextual political and other factors that it would be premature to focus on modeling before we understood the broader dimensions of the problem. Seminar-style gaming appeared to be the approach that would best enable us to bound the problem of anti-access threats and counters.

The conflict scenarios used in the study were designed to illuminate anti-access strategies and threats in peacetime, crisis, and war in four geographic areas of responsibility—European, Pacific, Central, and Southern Commands. We considered more than a dozen potential scenarios for our assessment, ultimately choosing scenarios according to three criteria.

The first was whether the scenario offered a good case for exploring the anti-access strategies that might be available to the most capable potential adversary in a region. The second was whether the scenario would thereby assist in identifying what might be considered "high-end" anti-access threats, enabling us to treat other instances as "lesser-included cases." The third was whether, in combination, the scenarios would present a reasonably rich range of contexts in which land forces might be deployed and employed. In constructing these scenarios, the study team occasionally sacrificed detail in areas that seemed less relevant to access issues to better illuminate the character of potential access challenges.

The result of this screening of potential scenarios led us to focus on three major regional scenarios—one each for Southwest Asia, the Western Pacific, and Northern Europe—and a somewhat less detailed consideration of a range of scenarios for Central and South America.[7]

We used the same basic approach for each game, first specifying the scenario in significant detail for consideration in seminar gaming. First, we posited a U.S. adversary ("Red") and likely members of its coalition, and the U.S. coalition ("Blue"), including those providing base access and transit rights. Next, we identified the political and military objectives for Blue and Red, as well as potential differences in objectives among coalition members that might constitute fault lines in the coalition. We identified Blue and Red concepts of operation, forces, and their likely deployment chains—including APOEs/SPOEs and APODs/SPODs and likely flightpaths or sea routes for U.S. forces and other forces—and notional operational schemes of maneuver. The results of these efforts were briefed to the study team as a whole at the beginning of each seminar game.

Because the focus of the study was access, in most cases[8] we did not undertake analyses of the results of combat in a military campaign. Rather, in the seminar games, we focused on the possible effectiveness of a wide range of plausible adversary efforts to deter, prevent, or degrade or delay the introduction of U.S. forces into the theater in light of Blue's available counters. We first identified potential "weak links" in the deployment chain, from CONUS to the theater of interest, where an adversary might profitably direct political, economic, or military actions that might thereby disrupt a U.S. deployment, and assessed the military and other capabilities of adversaries (or their proxies or allies) to successfully exploit vulnerabilities in this deployment chain in ways that could deter, prevent, or degrade or delay U.S. introduction of forces into the theater. As part

---

[7] Our view was that anti-access threats in Central and South America would generally be at the low end but that drug ties might give these groups relatively more substantial resources for acquiring capabilities than groups that did not benefit from this sort of high-risk, high-payoff illicit economic activity. For a recent analysis of the nexus between transnational crime and terrorism, see Geoffrey B. Demarest, "In Colombia—A Terrorist Sanctuary?" *Military Review*, March–April 2002, pp. 48–57.

[8] The only exception was spreadsheet-based campaign modeling of the potential operational impacts of Iranian closure of the Strait of Hormuz.

of this assessment, we notionally identified prioritized targets for the adversary. Finally, we identified Blue counters to these actions and performed a net assessment of the possible effectiveness of these counters in mitigating the anti-access threats we had earlier identified. These judgments were all made jointly by the study team—typically after lively debate and discussion—with each set of judgments (e.g., Blue vulnerabilities, Red methods, Blue counters) captured in a separate spreadsheet matrix, all of which were again considered in the context of an overall net assessment. Each scenario typically required two or three days for the study team to complete the seminar game.

The next four chapters document the main results of these games. Chapter Three reports the results of a game analyzing an Iraq crisis (the U.S. Central Command/U.S, Army Central Command area of responsibility [AOR]) premised on indications and warning of Iraq's imminent acquisition of a nuclear weapon. Chapter Four reports the results of a Russia-Baltics game (U.S. European Command/U.S. Army, Europe, AOR) premised on Russian concerns about NATO expansion and minority rights in Latvia, Lithuania, and Estonia. Chapter Five summarizes a game looking at a People's Republic of China (PRC)-Taiwan crisis (U.S. Pacific Command/ U.S. Army, Pacific, AOR) premised on growing PRC impatience over the status of Taiwan. Chapter Six summarizes the results of our consideration of a range of scenarios relating to Central and South America (U.S. Southern Command/U. S. Army South).

CHAPTER THREE

Southwest Asian Theater: An Iraq Game

This chapter details our gaming of an Iraq scenario. We begin with an overview of the game and a description of the scenario, the actors and their objectives, concepts of operations (CONOPs), and capabilities. We then summarize our findings by detailing key access issues suggested by the scenario, the anti-access threats of greatest concern, and other threats we considered. We conclude by summarizing the implications for regional commanders regarding access requirements and other issues, and options that are available to reduce the efficacy of regional anti-access strategies. The chapter concludes with a brief description of the implications of our campaign simulation modeling of an Iranian attempt to close the Strait of Hormuz.

Overview of the Game

The Southwest Asia (SWA) anti-access scenario provided a context for exploring Iraqi, U.S., and Gulf Cooperation Council (GCC) objectives, strategies, CONOPs, and capabilities in the U.S. Central Command (CENTCOM) area of responsibility in two time frames (2003–2007 and 2012). In developing this scenario, the study team conducted a net assessment of Iraqi anti-access capabilities against the entire U.S. deployment chain—including homeland (CONUS), en-route, and in-theater threats—and identified signposts and wild cards that should be monitored.

The Scenario

An Iraqi scenario was chosen to explore the difficult access environment that might be encountered in the Persian Gulf. As general background for the scenario, we postulated that under the leadership of Saddam Hussein Iraq was believed to be within three to six months of developing a nuclear weapons capability.[1]

Working through international institutions, the United States unsuccessfully pressed Iraq to allow the return of UN weapons inspectors, warning Iraq that if it did not allow the return of the UN inspectors, the United States would take "appropriate action" to deal with the imminent danger posed by the Iraqi nuclear weapons program. The international community was posited to waver in its support of the United States, arguing that Saddam should be given more time to comply. In particular, fearful of becoming a target of Iraqi nuclear weapons, Saudi Arabia warned the United States that it would not support U.S. military strikes against Iraq. Russia, Germany, and France indicated that they would not support the United States by providing military forces. On the other hand, Great Britain "stood firm" in its support of nonproliferation and the global war against terrorism.

---

[1] "DIA (Defense Intelligence Agency) Testimony to Select Committee on Intelligence: Worldwide Threat to US National Security Interests," available at http://www.security management.com/library/000255.html, accessed February 22, 2002; "Foreign Missile Developments and the Ballistic Missile Threat Through 2015," Central Intelligence Agency, available at http://www.cia.gov/nic/pubs/other_products/Unclassifiedballisticmissilefinal. html, accessed January 10, 2002; Kathleen C. Bailey, "Iraq's Asymmetric Threat to the United States and U.S. Allies," *Comparative Strategy*, Vol. 21, 2002, pp. 161–177; *Iraq's Weapons of Mass Destruction—The Assessment of the British Government*, printed circa October 2002 from http://www.fco.gov.uk/Files/kfile/iraqdossier.pdf; The White House, *A Decade of Deception and Defiance—Saddam Hussein's Defiance of the United Nations*, printed circa September 2002 from http://www.whitehouse.gov/news/releases/2002/09/20020912. html; Robert Shuey, "Nuclear, Biological, and Chemical Weapons and Missiles: The Current Situation and Trends," *CRS Report for Congress*, RL30699, August 10, 2001, pp. 1–30.

Unlike many other SWA scenarios, ours assumed that U.S. and coalition forces were denied access to preferred Saudi infrastructure.[2] Saudi Arabia's failure to join the coalition had the potential of dislocating the U.S. campaign plan, necessitating amphibious assaults to secure a lodgment, use of alternative host nation support (e.g., Jordan, Turkey), or both. Without Saudi infrastructure, deploying U.S. and coalition forces would have fewer SPODs and APODs available, resulting in congestion and increased travel distances to the combat zone. If Iraq invaded Kuwait, however, we believe it most likely that Saudi Arabia would provide access. If an invasion took place during a period of Saudi internal crisis and instability, the outcome would be, at best, indeterminate.

This region seemed particularly susceptible to strategic distraction—e.g., by "playing the Israel card," destabilizing governments friendly to U.S. interests, and escalating the conflict vertically or horizontally (e.g., by using weapons of mass destruction or bringing other Arab states or Iran into the conflict). Iran also was a significant anti-access wild card in this scenario. We believed that under some circumstances Iran might warn that it would "defend itself against Western aggression" and take a hostile position toward the United States, thereby complicating the military action against Iraq. Thus, the U.S.-led coalition needed to be continually on guard against the possibility that a potentially hostile Iran might threaten or act to close the Strait of Hormuz.[3]

Another aspect of this case study was that it relied extensively on the synergy of a joint, combined-arms force (consisting of land, maritime, and air components) to counter anti-access strategies and methods that included ballistic, cruise, surface-to-air, and antiship missiles, sea mines, etc. Additionally, the scenario broached the possibility that

---

[2] The scenario was constructed in early 2002.

[3] Because of the significant potential for mischief presented by the Strait of Hormuz, we also undertook a spreadsheet-based analysis of the impact on campaign outcomes of an Iranian closure of the Strait of Hormuz, undertaken in concert with an Iranian invasion of Kuwait and Saudi Arabia.

Army forces might need to be deployed directly into a combat zone and required to undertake forced-entry or assault operations.

Actors, Objectives, CONOPs, and Capabilities

Iraqi Objectives, CONOPs, and Capabilities. Saddam Hussein's theater objectives center on denying the United States access by fostering international and regional resentment toward U.S. actions against Iraq, particularly in the Arab world. Other diplomatic efforts include a mixture of military, diplomatic, and economic coercion directed at weakening the resolve of the GCC states, including Kuwait, to grant the United States access in a future conflict. Saddam also fuels Israeli-Palestinian discord to tie down and distract the U.S. and international community. Finally, Iraq attempts to loosen or eliminate remaining UN sanctions.

Iraq employs a total of 23 divisions, including 17 regular army divisions (six armored/mechanized and 11 infantry) and six Republican Guard divisions (four armored/mechanized and two infantry), as well as about 60 helicopters and a composite air force of 70-plus tactical aircraft. Iraq is posited to have an integrated air defense system (IADS) with hardened command and control (C2) systems and recourse to special operations forces (SOF) and terrorist capabilities.

The scenario assumes that, to maintain Saudi neutrality and thereby compound U.S. access difficulties, Iraqi forces will not invade Kuwait. Iraq would, however, mine Kuwaiti waters and employ antiship missiles to prevent coalition sea access to Kuwait. Iraq might also consider establishing a surface-to-air missile (SAM) umbrella over Kuwait to thwart the U.S.-led air campaign and prevent the deployment of coalition forces to Kuwait by air. This, however, would require longer-range SAMs than are currently in the Iraqi inventory.

Although we thought it unlikely that Iraq would actually use WMD, we believed that Iraq could threaten the use of WMD and "environmental terrorism" to deter access and to raise the risks of concentrating coalition forces, particularly in Kuwait.[4] Iraq targets

---

[4] Theodore Karasik, *Toxic Warfare*, Santa Monica, Calif.: RAND Corporation, MR-1572-AF, 2002.

Kuwaiti APODs/SPODs with ballistic and cruise missiles and long-range fires while using longer range Scuds against Bahrain and Qatar. Israel is also a likely target of the Scud launches. Saddam continues to fuel the Israeli-Palestinian conflict as a strategic distraction for the U.S.-led coalition.

Once engaged with U.S. and coalition forces, Iraq attempts to conduct a war of attrition by inflicting the maximum number of casualties possible and prolonging the conflict to stalemate, thus weakening the resolve of the U.S.-led coalition and bringing international pressures to bear. Saddam's ultimate objective is to preserve his power and regime.

In the air portion of the conflict, Iraq employs its IADS to combat and negate the U.S.-led air campaign. On the ground, the Iraqi CONOP is to draw coalition forces into strong defensive belts and strong points centered on military operations in urban terrain environments, including a final house-to-house last stand in Baghdad. In such circumstances, Iraq might use WMD and environmental disaster to slow down and inflict casualties on coalition forces and cause maximum collateral damage even on its own territory.

Iraq also continues to pursue opportunities for strategic distraction by encouraging horizontal escalation (e.g., Israel and Iran). Ballistic missiles are the weapon of choice. Also at the strategic level, with the onset of hostilities, we posited a modest revision of the Iraqi objectives. Iraq seeks continued sympathy in the Arab world while fostering discord and dissension between the United States and its European allies. Iraq also capitalizes on Iranian suspicions of U.S. intent in the Gulf region and attempts to bring Iran into the conflict as a cobelligerent. Iranian entry would eliminate the focus on Iraq, dilute the coalition military effort, and compound U.S. access difficulties because of Iran's advantageous geographical position at the Straits of Hormuz.

Iraq practices a defense in depth with three primary defensive belts extending from the Euphrates River to the Iranian border. Each of these defensive belts would in turn consist of several defensive lines, each with an extensive system of entrenchments, fortifications, and minefields. Strong points would be positioned in urban centers.

The Iraqis would fortify Basra, leaving it as a thorn in the side of the projected coalition advance deeper inside Iraq. Reminiscent of Hitler and Berlin in 1945, Saddam and the Republican Guard would make a last stand in Baghdad itself, hoping to inflame Arab opinion about collateral damage and civilian losses.[5] Finally, Saddam would keep a watchful eye and likely suppress any indigenous opposition to his regime.[6]

Wild cards for this scenario included the potential early Iraqi use of WMD, and the potential U.S. reaction to such an event.[7] Iraqi use of WMD against targets in Israel could have changed the situation considerably. We also considered the world and GCC reaction to Iraqi "environmental terrorism," including the destruction of oilfields and spilling oil into the Persian Gulf, as having the potential to alter the military situation. Iraqi SOF operations, particularly those carried out by surrogates and terrorists using chemical, biological, radiological, nuclear, or high explosive (CBRNE) weapons, might have the potential to cause paralysis, get the coalition to waiver, or result in otherwise unforeseeable consequences. Iranian entry into the conflict also could alter the military balance—and exacerbate the access problem—dramatically and shift the military and political situation in unpredictable ways.

U.S. and Allied Objectives, CONOPS, and Capabilities. The SWA scenario postulated four significant U.S. peacetime theater objectives. Primary among these is the need for the United States to gain control of or eliminate Iraqi nuclear WMD and delivery capabilities. The second objective is to build and maintain coalition support, with a mind to further future access in the region. The third is

---

[5] Our military operations in urban terrain analysis is drawn from numerous RAND sources, including Russell Glenn et al., *Ready for Armageddon: Proceedings of the 2001 RAND Arroyo-Joint ACTD-CETO-USMC Nonlethal and Urban Operations Program Urban Operations Conference*, Santa Monica, Calif.: RAND Corporation, CF-179-A, 2002.

[6] This opposition could come in many forms, either tribal (within the Baath party) or religious (Sunnis, Shias, and Christians).

[7] For example, L-29 drones could provide a capability for dispensing chemical or biological agents. See Joby Warrick, "Iraqi Drones May be Used to Spread Death," *Washington Post*, September 6, 2002, available at http://www.washingtonpost.com.

to remove Saddam Hussein from power through covert operations and support to regime opponents, replacing Saddam with a more Western-friendly government while maintaining Iraqi territorial integrity. The final U.S. objective is to maintain stable oil prices by ensuring the flow of oil from the Persian Gulf.

The United States deploys an early-entry joint force package that includes a brigade combat team (BCT); air defense capabilities consisting of naval, Patriot PAC-3, and theater high-altitude area defense (THAAD) batteries; an attack helicopter battalion; Multiple-Launch Rocket System (MLRS) and Army Tactical Missile System (ATACMS); a Marine Expeditionary Unit (MEU); prepositioning ships and cargo handling and terminal operations personnel; two carrier battle groups and a command ship; and a USAF air expeditionary task force to supplement air forces already in the theater. In total, the United States deploys an Army armored division and mechanized infantry division from V Corps as well as an air assault division and infantry division from XVIII Airborne Corps, a Marine Expeditionary Force (MEF), attack helicopters, MLRS/ATACMS, a Ranger battalion, and a Special Forces group. Naval elements include three carrier battle groups, three amphibious ready groups, two maritime prepositioning squadrons, four minesweepers, a command-and-control ship, and P-3 surveillance and EA-6B jamming aircraft. The Air Force contribution includes 30 long-range bombers, about four wings of tactical combat aircraft, E-3 Airborne Warning and Control System (AWACS) aircraft, E-8 Joint Surveillance and Target Attack Radar System (JSTARS) aircraft, RC-135s, Global Hawk unmanned aerial vehicles (UAVs), tankers, and other supporting aircraft. The British are posited to contribute an armored division and a wing of Tornado strike aircraft, and three brigades of forces are posited to come from Kuwait, with another brigade from the other GCC states. The GCC states also are posited to contribute a number of F-16s, F/A-18s, and other aircraft.

In our scenario, we assumed that the Gulf states of Oman, Qatar, Bahrain, Kuwait, and the United Arab Emirates (UAE) support the United States with access to bases and military forces. Turkey also provides access and bases, thereby providing a "Northern

Option" for the coalition partners. Great Britain also provides bases and is the only coalition partner to contribute significant military forces. Remaining neutral in this SWA scenario are Saudi Arabia, Jordan, Syria, and Yemen. Egypt quietly allows the U.S. overflights and use of the Suez Canal but does not permit the use of its bases.

In brief, the U.S. and allied CONOP posited by the study team is, first, to covertly insert SOF capabilities to assist the Iraqi opposition and pin down Iraqi forces in northern Iraq while establishing air superiority over Iraq, and littoral control. Next, air strikes would be conducted against Iraqi C2, air defense, ballistic missile launchers, and subsequently against Iraqi lines of communication and ground forces. Forces are staged in Kuwait and Turkey, and Iraq is invaded by ground forces that drive to Baghdad, remove Saddam from power, and occupy Iraq until a new government can be formed.

Findings

To summarize, our analysis of Iraqi threats and U.S. and coalition vulnerabilities concluded that for the period considered Iraq will be unable to prevent U.S. access or delay or degrade U.S. mission-capable forces enough to prevent them from accomplishing their missions satisfactorily.

Key Access Issues

In-Theater Access Issues. Denied the use of Saudi Arabia's constellation of ports and airfields, the U.S. military is essentially restricted to one airfield (Kuwait IAP) and one port (Shuaiba) in Kuwait through which to deploy its forces.[8] While both of these installations are well

---

[8] Saudi Arabia's unwillingness to support this operation will also cause problems for the U.S. Army's prepositioning program. Currently, APS-5 has a Brigade Set, a Division Base, and sustainment stocks stored in Qatar as well as two hospitals in Bahrain. Because neither of these countries shares a land border with Kuwait, this equipment must be moved by sea or air forward into a potentially hostile zone. This problem is further complicated by the shallowness of both of Qatar's ports, which cannot accommodate fully loaded Large

suited for strategic deployment operations, no excess capacity elsewhere can be readily used in case either of them is seized or damaged.
This reliance on just two major ports of debarkation (PODs) in
Kuwait is the primary weakness in the U.S. deployment chain and
provides Iraq with its best opportunity to use its limited military anti-
access options to delay or prevent the deployment of U.S. personnel
and equipment. Additional APODs and SPODs are available in other
friendly Gulf emirates, but none is linked by land to Kuwait, necessitating complex transshipment operations if they are to be used.

This limited availability of PODs in Kuwait is the primary
potential weakness in the U.S. deployment chain. If Iraq can shut
down either Kuwait IAP or Shuaiba for any length of time, the U.S.
deployment will slow to a trickle. Both of Kuwait's other airfields, Ali
al Salem AB and Ahmed al Jaber AB, have very limited capacities to
support lift operations. Kuwait's other port, Shuwaikh, is too shallow
to accept large lift ships, thus leaving the only viable alternative to
Shuaiba a Joint Logistics over-the-Shore (JLOTS) operation. This is a
lengthy process that can be highly dependent on the weather and
prevailing sea states. As a result, the extremely limited robustness of
Kuwait's deployment infrastructure gives Iraq an opportunity to use
creative tactics (supported by luck) to bring U.S. deployment
operations in Kuwait to a standstill. Given the high payoff to Iraq of
closing either Shuaiba or Kuwait IAP, the United States should be on
the alert for creative or unconventional Iraqi tactics to shut them
down.

The lack of access to fighter bases close to Iraq offers the potential to seriously degrade the operations tempo of U.S. tactical air
strikes against Iraqi targets. Sortie rates begin to drop dramatically for
missions longer than 800 nautical miles.[9] As a result, a combination
of access denial and regional air base structural limitations that neces-
sitates the use of additional airfields at greater ranges from potential

---

Medium-Speed Roll-On/Roll-Off ships (LMSRs). As a result, the equipment must be
transshipped by sea in partially loaded vessels.

[9] William D. O'Malley, *Evaluating Possible Airfield Deployment Options: Middle East Contingencies,* Santa Monica, Calif.: RAND Corporation, MR-1353, 2001, pp. 22–23.

targets might have a pronounced effect on USAF and joint operations.

Two potential challenges are associated with the use of prepositioned material in this scenario. First, because Qatar lacks a contiguous land border with Kuwait, the APS-5 equipment stored there must be moved forward by sea to Kuwait. This operation will be hampered by the inability of Qatar's ports to accommodate fully-loaded LMSRs and by the lack of U.S. lift ships deployed to the region. In this scenario we envision using the LMSRs from APS-3 to shuttle the Qatar-based equipment forward. Normally, this would require about 2.5 *Watson*-class LMSR missions, but, given the draft restrictions at Umm Said, additional missions may be required. This necessity is not a "show-stopper," but it does increase the time necessary to bring these forces to bear on Iraq. Normally, the U.S. Army would plan to have APS-3 ready for action within 96 hours after the arrival of the main body of troops from CONUS. However, with the necessity of waiting for APS-3 to unload, it may be at least three weeks before the Qatar-based equipment is combat-ready.

En-Route Access Issues. The sea lanes to Kuwait from CONUS, Europe, and Diego Garcia have four potential chokepoints: the Strait of Gibraltar, the Suez Canal, Bab el Mandeb, and the Strait of Hormuz (see figure 3.1). Although it is unlikely that Iraq could interdict U.S. lift ships en route, it is at these points that Iraqi attacks by SOF or irregular forces would have the greatest chances of success.

The primary en-route weak point is the Suez Canal. U.S. lift ships traveling by this route will be transiting through potentially unfriendly territory and will be vulnerable to innovative Iraqi tactics, such as the use of block ships, mines, or SOF and guerrilla attacks. These potential vulnerabilities will mean that use of the canal may depend to a large degree on the extent and willingness of the Egyptian government to provide security for U.S. vessels using it.

Because of denied transit rights throughout much of the region—and especially Saudi Arabia—lift aircraft must fly a circuitous route, consuming time and fuel and fostering a need for alternative basing. The most important en-route bases are RAF Akrotiri

Figure 3.1
Sea Routes for a Deployment to the Kuwait Theater of Operations

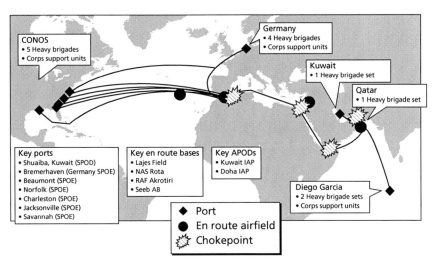

CONOS
• 5 Heavy brigades
• Corps support units

Germany
• 4 Heavy brigades
• Corps support units

Kuwait
• 1 Heavy brigade set

Qatar
• 1 Heavy brigade set

Key ports
• Shuaiba, Kuwait (SPOD)
• Bremerhaven (Germany SPOE)
• Beaumont (SPOE)
• Norfolk (SPOE)
• Charleston (SPOE)
• Jacksonville (SPOE)
• Savannah (SPOE)

Key en route bases
• Lajes Field
• NAS Rota
• RAF Akrotiri
• Seeb AB

Key APODs
• Kuwait IAP
• Doha IAP

Diego Garcia
• 2 Heavy brigade sets
• Corps support units

◆ Port
● En route airfield
✺ Chokepoint

on Cyprus and Seeb in Oman because they are necessary for the diversion around denied Saudi airspace. Prepositioned equipment in Kuwait and elsewhere in the region and afloat prepositioned material both would significantly speed up the deployment of U.S. forces.

Iran's reaction to this operation also is an important wild card in this scenario. Were it to be actively hostile, deployment operations would become much more difficult because of its potential ability to close the Strait of Hormuz and the threat it can pose to strategic lift assets transiting through or over the Persian Gulf. Even if Iran remains passively hostile, the United States may be required to escort strategic lift ships and aircraft through the region and divert significant military assets, including command, control, communications, intelligence, surveillance, and reconnaissance (C3ISR) and battle management aircraft, to guard against a sudden entrance of Iran into the conflict on the side of Iraq.

CONUS Access Issues. The anti-access study team viewed the possibility of an attack on CONUS as unlikely because of Iraq's lack of strategic reach and the difficulty it would have in inserting SOF or irregular forces into the United States. In any case, such an attack would be unlikely to have a direct military effect, and its impacts would be largely psychological.

Threats of Greatest Concern

Iraq's conventional military weakness over the near to medium term leaves Iraq with a very finite set of tools with which it can threaten U.S. access to the Persian Gulf before and during a conventional war.

Our assessment of homeland, en-route, and theater deployment chain vulnerabilities, military threat assessment, and Blue counters indicated that in-theater information operations (IO) and psychological operations (PSYOPS), intermediate-range ballistic missile (IRBM) and short-range ballistic missile (SRBM) attacks, armored and mechanized forces, and terrorist CBRNE attacks were the anti-access threats of greatest concern for an Iraq scenario. Iraq's greatest threat is the use of IO and PSYOPS to exploit U.S. missteps in the region with the "Arab street." Although Iraq does not have a particularly good PSYOPS capability, the nature of the opportunities that exist in the region and Saddam Hussein's ability to exploit media attention make this likely the central threat to U.S. access.[10]

Information and Psychological Operations. The threat of IO and PSYOPS was assessed to be all the greater in our scenario precisely because of Iraq's military weakness. Appeals to pan-Arab solidarity and propaganda videos of the hardships endured by Iraqi civilians as a result of U.S. air strikes and UN sanctions would be underwritten by Scud missile attacks against Israel aimed at compelling Israel to enter the war against Iraq. These measures could be used to try to fracture whatever international coalition Washington can muster in this scenario. We have noted in our analysis that Iraqi PSYOPS capability is not of high quality but also argue that it does not need to be because in the highly charged anti-American atmosphere that permeates much of the Arab world, even very mediocre

---

[10] PSYOPS activities could include cyber warfare, including email and graffiti or defacing of web pages. See Giles Trendle, "Cyberwars: The Coming Arab E-Jihad," *The Middle East*, April 2002, pp. 5–8.

PSYOPS efforts by the Iraqis could result in a payoff, particularly in light of the ongoing conflict between Israel and the Palestinians.

Conventional and Unconventional Military Threats. In terms of Iraqi anti-access threats of a military nature, we deemed that the prospect of a conventional ground invasion of Kuwait, IRBM and SRBM attacks against the Kuwaiti APOD/SPOD, and CBRNE attacks against U.S. military installations in the Persian Gulf would be of greatest concern in our scenario to the commander of CENT-COM.[11] It should be emphasized that all of Iraq's standard military anti-access options are in-theater—Iraq simply does not have the strategic reach to offer a serious or sustained threat to the U.S. en-route infrastructure.

Conventional Ground Forces. Although Iraqi ground forces remained weak after the heavy damage they suffered in Desert Storm, the Republican Guard divisions were still more than strong enough to overrun Kuwait if they could accomplish a surprise attack. The permanent U.S. one-brigade presence in Kuwait would likely not be enough to decisively halt such an Iraqi move. If Iraq were to overrun Kuwait in our scenario, and Saudi Arabia remained neutral, it would make a U.S. attack from the south very difficult because the United States would probably need to mount an amphibious invasion of Kuwait from bases in Qatar just to reacquire a jumping off point for a southern invasion. However, the consensus of our team was that Saudi Arabia would quickly grant the United States access to its military infrastructure if the Iraqis actually invaded Kuwait. This would largely solve the U.S. access problem in the theater.

Ballistic Missiles. Because Kuwait has only one suitable APOD and SPOD, the Iraqis could conceivably try to deny U.S. access to the theater by launching a barrage attack with most of their remaining Scud inventory to damage either facility so heavily that it would have to temporarily shut down or try to launch a series of attacks to

---

[11] That said, the study team concluded that Iraq probably would be restrained, at least initially, in the use of WMD, in order to achieve maximum leverage from its IO/PSYOPS campaign.

suppress operations. If a conventional barrage attack were beyond the capacity of the Iraqis (which may well be the case), they could try to use a handful of Scuds with chemical warheads to accomplish the same ends. A chemical attack would be most effective if persistent nerve agents were employed.

Iraq's ballistic missile inventory would be preferentially targeted on Kuwait. Militarily, Iraq could interrupt the deployment by terrorizing port and airfield workers, possibly with a WMD payload. Iraqi use of IRBM/SRBM probably depends on availability of submunitions, because the Global Positioning System (GPS) probably would not be an option available to Iraq.[12] Iraq would need improved guidance (e.g., terminal radar guidance and maneuverable warheads) to achieve higher accuracy. Our analysis also assumed either improved accuracy or WMD payload, plus increased missile inventories to underwrite a missile campaign over time. Iraq may have 75–125 ballistic missiles capable of reaching the ports of Kuwait.

Finally, unless its missile accuracy, C2, and ISR capabilities improve or its long-range systems are made capable of accommodating payloads with area effects (e.g., submunitions, mines, chemical and biological payloads), Iraq's principal aim probably would be to achieve psychological/strategic impacts rather than expecting its attacks to destroy specific military targets. We acknowledged, however, the possibility of using ballistic missiles either in a campaign with a strategic or psychological focus or in one that sought to maximize military impacts.

Military actions consistent with a strategic or psychological focus would include

- strategic attacks on Israel or Jordan, or elimination of opposition enclaves;

---

[12] Our assumption was that Iraqi access to GPS data that would allow a tight circular error probable (CEP) for its missiles probably would remain unavailable and detectable on the global arms market, both legal and black. If this assumption were proved wrong, more accurate targeting would be possible.

- attacks on personnel-rich targets (e.g., the combined air operations center at Al Udeid, Qatar, barracks) to affect "will" and disrupt C2; and
- harassment of Gulf APODs and SPODs (e.g., in Qatar and Bahrain) or other GCC targets (e.g., UAE, Oman) to disrupt deployment-related operations and terrorize civilian workers.

In aiming for military anti-access impacts, Iraq probably would allocate attacks against such targets as the following (although in some cases Iraqi forces would need to use more effective, shorter-range systems—e.g., SOF, mines):

- Kuwaiti APODs/SPODs, which are critical to the U.S. buildup.
- Other high-payoff targets, such as an LMSR with equipment or land-based prepositioning stocks whose loss could delay or degrade the buildup of forces or an ammo ship in a port whose loss could degrade operations.

CBRNE Attacks. One wild card in the threat area in this scenario is the possibility of CBRNE attacks against American military installations throughout the Persian Gulf region. The probability of such attacks and their likely impact is very difficult to assess because both would depend on the skill of covert Iraqi SOF units or the ability of the Iraqis to contract out such asymmetric attacks to nonstate terrorist groups. Our analysis indicated that a CBRNE event would have the potential to delay or degrade the buildup of significant mission-capable forces. However, measuring the potential impact of such an event depends on too many variables, such as size and number, which makes the likelihood of Iraqi use of CBRNE difficult to assess.

Finally, it is worth noting that threats of greatest concern are additive, meaning that if Iraq directed multiple anti-access threats against APODs/SPODs, the net result could be a significant problem. The limited robustness of available ports and airfields (limited in this scenario to Kuwait) makes the region extremely vulnerable to anti-access measures. The probability of a successful attack may not be high, but a high payoff would occur if it were successful.

Other Threats Considered

Several other threats seemed less likely to us, but bear mentioning.

Sea Mining. Iraqi ability to place sea mines in or near Kuwait waters is minimal. Iraq would most likely place these mines covertly using modified merchant ships, the ubiquitous dhow, or small, high-speed boats. The military impact of Iraqi use of sea mines would be to slow the deployment of U.S. forces while waiting for mine clearance. A "lucky" Iraqi hit on a major U.S. ship (e.g., worst case of LMSR) could have severe operational impact. However, current in-theater U.S. mine countermeasures (MCM) capabilities are sufficient to deal with any possible Iraqi sea mines threat.

Special Operations Forces. Iraq could get a lucky hit on a high-value U.S. target if it developed more substantial SOF capabilities, but the chances of either this or sea-mining are remote. The most likely SOF targets would be APODs/SPODs or economic, political, and other "soft" targets (e.g., desalinization plants, oilfields, oil pipelines) and targets chosen to terrorize or induce strategic paralysis. Oil fires might degrade APOD/SPOD and air operations.

Integrated Air Defense System. Iraqi IADS could not influence the flow of forces into Gulf APODs, but could hinder U.S. efforts to stop a quick land grab against Kuwait by providing additional protective cover to Iraqi ground forces.

Implications for Regional Commanders

Access Requirements

The SWA scenario we have posited in this report requires the commander of CENTCOM to carry out three major tasks to successfully obtain and maintain the theater access required to execute the kind of CONOPs that would have a high probability of overthrowing the Saddam regime in Iraq. The three principal requirements are

- acquiring diplomatic permissions to use a sufficient number of combat air bases within 800 nautical miles of Iraq to mount a sustained air campaign;

- securing the main APOD and SPOD in Kuwait against any kind of Iraqi attack; and
- ensuring the free flow of maritime military traffic through the key en-route chokepoints that guard the entrance to the Persian Gulf theater.

Each will be discussed.

Acquiring Diplomatic Permissions. The absence of Saudi Arabia as a staging area for American forces in this scenario creates a potential maximum on ground (MOG) aircraft and ramp space problem for U.S. ground-based tactical air units in the Persian Gulf. Although the relatively small tactical fighter aircraft (F-15, F-16, F-117, etc.) do not take up large amounts of space, the enabling air assets that would support them in any sustained air campaign over Iraq (AWACS, JSTARS, Compass Call, etc.) tend to be larger and, accordingly, have more substantial ramp space requirements. The theater commander can mitigate this problem somewhat through an increased reliance on carrier-based aircraft and long-range bombers based on Diego Garcia and in CONUS. A further measure that could be taken would be to maximize the number of Joint Direct-Attack Munition–capable land-based tactical aircraft deployed to the theater because this might enable the Joint Force Air Component Commander to trade off some quantity while maintaining the quality of the land-based tactical air fleet being assembled. These mitigating measures notwithstanding, the United States will need access to most of the air bases in the small Persian Gulf emirates and at least one or two bases in Turkey to conduct a sustained air campaign. At minimum, bases in Qatar, the UAE, and Bahrain would be needed to complement the bases used in Kuwait. Bases for longer-range aircraft in Oman (bombers, P-3s, AC-130s, F-15Es) would be helpful but probably are not indispensable.[13]

---

[13] USAF thinkers are currently exploring the idea of having an air expeditionary force deploy to multiple bases as a way of foiling enemy theater ballistic missiles (TBMs), SOF, and other long-range strikes. Adoption of this tactic would lead to a requirement for additional

Securing APODs/SPODs. Securing the APOD and SPOD in Kuwait is the sine qua non of success in our SWA scenario. This is because the bulk of the ground force invasion of Iraq must be mounted and sustained from Kuwaiti territory and because the single SPOD and single APOD in that country will serve as the end of the deployment chain for ground forces from CONUS. Any disruption of the operation of either facility could dramatically slow the marshaling and onward movement process for U.S. ground forces. The theater combatant commander can deal with this problem in two ways, which are not mutually exclusive. First, he can set up a covering force to physically guard Kuwait against any surprise Iraqi ground or TBM barrage attack. Such a force would likely include a heavy brigade positioned along the border with Iraq, a force of attack aircraft on call from bases throughout the Persian Gulf, and an anti-TBM shield made up of Patriot and THAAD batteries. This kind of covering force probably must rely on innovative tactics to defeat any Iraqi attack, likely including the generous use of deep-fire capabilities, such as MLRS batteries and Apache attack helicopters. Some passive defense measures to harden the APOD (e.g., more concrete shelters, collective protection, chemical decontamination stations) and development of rapid repair capabilities could be undertaken. Second, the commander could seek to preempt any spoiling attack on Kuwait by carrying out a rolling-start offensive in which the U.S. air campaign would begin, at least at a low level, before major ground force equipment sets have begun to move from CONUS and from regional prepositioning sites into the theater and afloat prepositioning ships. A rolling-start air campaign could commence with just the air assets the United States has permanently on station in the Persian Gulf.

Ensuring the Free Flow of Maritime Traffic into the Theater. The third task of securing the en-route maritime chokepoints is probably the least demanding, but, all the same, it should not be ignored. A small likelihood exists that Iraqi SOF or terrorists that have been hired by Iraq could try (using suicide boat attacks or covert

---

deployment airfields, which might be difficult to acquire in a theater constrained the way SWA is in our scenario.

mining) to interdict the flow of U.S. military cargo shipping through the Suez Canal, Strait of Hormuz, or Gulf of Aden. In the case of Suez and Aden, the solution is straightforward: establish close cooperative arrangements with friendly security forces in Yemen and Egypt. The Strait of Hormuz is more problematic because Iran controls the northern shore of that chokepoint and would almost certainly not be friendly toward the United States during our SWA scenario.[14] Large naval exercises along the Iranian coast could suffice as a deterrent against active Iranian support of any covert Iraqi campaign to interdict the flow of U.S. military cargo vessels.

Requirements of Allies. In addition to the requirements for a successful campaign just described, a number of requirements for U.S. partners and allies obtain. The United States would depend on allies in this contingency much more for basing access and rights than for actual military capability. In the latter area, the United States would certainly benefit from the participation of a British armored division and some British Tornado aircraft but could achieve its military objectives even in the absence of those technologically advanced and well-trained allied forces. However, absolutely indispensable for the U.S. cause in this scenario would be access to air bases, ports, and marshaling areas for ground forces in Kuwait, Bahrain, Qatar, the UAE, and Oman. Access to bases in Jordan and southeastern Turkey would be very useful as well, at the very least for combat search and rescue and SOF operations. Blanket access to facilities in these two states would enable the United States to expand its CONOPs options by conducting air base seizures, heliborne assaults, and feints in northern and western Iraq. Lastly, the United States would probably need some access to en-route Air Mobility Command (AMC) bases in Spain, the Azores, and Italy in order to build a cohesive airlift chain from CONUS to the Persian Gulf. En-route intermediate staging bases in Germany and Britain would be useful here but probably not absolutely necessary.

---

[14] Indeed, although it seemed unlikely that Iran would act in sympathy with Iraq, Iran could use antiship missiles, sea mines, diesel submarines, or all three to threaten U.S. ships entering the Gulf.

Options for Commander, CENTCOM

Over the mid- to long-term, a number of political and technological options exist that the commander of CENTCOM could develop to deal with scenarios similar to the Iraq case we studied in this project.

Political-Military. At the political level, it is imperative that extensive military-to-military and political-military contacts between CENTCOM and key Gulf militaries and governments continue and perhaps even grow. These contacts should include joint exercises, military educational exchanges, and detailed staff talks. In crises and conflicts, the types of relationships built through these peacetime programs will help the United States gain diplomatic access rights even when the regional climate is inflamed with anti-American sentiment on the "Arab street."

Military-Technical. At the purely military and technical levels, several measures could be taken in the mid- to long-term to help preserve and expand American access in SWA during peacetime, crisis, and actual conflict.

In peacetime, four measures appear beneficial.

First, despite its small area, a more robust military infrastructure could be built in Kuwait. Even if the Iraq threat passes in the next couple of years, the potential for a conflict between the United States and Iran remains and, in such a conflict, Kuwait would be a very important forward staging base for U.S. forces.[15] The construction of a second SPOD and APOD in Kuwait at greater strategic depth (i.e., closer to the Saudi border) would help make the deployment infrastructure much less vulnerable to the kinds of inaccurate SRBM/IRBM attacks likely to emanate from rogue states in the region.

Second, CENTCOM could benefit from the acquisition of more high-speed sealift—e.g., Theater Support Vessels (TSVs), to be based in the theater. High-speed military cargo vessels would be invaluable in allowing CENTCOM to shuttle equipment and sustainment stocks from rear area facilities in Qatar to Kuwait in situations where access to Saudi Arabia is proscribed. TSVs would allow

---

[15] Note, however, that Kuwait might be less willing to support the U.S. in a war with Iran.

the immediate start of deployment operations and enable the use of shallower, less developed ports in Kuwait, thus reducing congestion at ports unloading afloat prepositioning ships and maritime positioning ships arriving from Diego Garcia. In addition, because TSVs are smaller and can unload more quickly than LMSRs, they present both a quicker and less valuable target to Iraqi (or other) strike planners, thus reducing the probability that they will be targeted by Iraq's limited SRBM stocks. Other possible measures would be to forward-deploy the current generation of logistics support vessels in-theater, to charter regional ferries or car carriers, or to convince Qatar to deepen its berths at either Umm Said or Doha. Because of the proximity of Camp Doha (the APS-5 site in Kuwait) to the Iraqi border and its relatively unhardened state, there is a small risk that the equipment stored there could be destroyed either by Iraqi long-range weapon systems or innovative Iraqi tactics. The probability of success for such an operation is low, but it has a high payoff for Iraq because it could destroy a large amount of difficult to replace equipment.

Third, CENTCOM should explore the possibility of creating specialized, joint, forced-entry packages that could reduce the need for multiple fixed bases in friendly Gulf countries by having a capability to rapidly move into enemy territory to seize lodgments and bare-bones APODs that could then be upgraded and used to receive forces directly from CONUS. This kind of capability would seem to be a logical progression forward from the capability demonstrated by the USMC in the Objective Rhino campaign during the Afghan War.

Fourth, it would be appropriate to develop and test technologies that would improve U.S. ability to deploy forces over the shore when all major SPODs in the theater were heavily damaged. This could involve innovative use of vertical lift, lighterage, high-speed sealift, and perhaps even floating sea bases or dirigibles.[16]

In time of crisis, we believe that the emergence of the rapidly deployable Stryker Brigade Combat Team (SBCT) capability in the

---

[16] One of our reviewers was skeptical that dirigibles might play a role in this scenario unless they were coming from Qatar. The superior cost-effectiveness of such a concept relative to other available alternatives would need to be established to justify pursuing such a program.

Army raises the prospect that robust Army forces may soon be available for creative deterrence operations in the Persian Gulf during a crisis. SBCTs are not designed for close combat with heavy armored forces, such as those in the Iraqi Republican Guard, but they do have enough of a punch to give pause to regional aggressors if used in a creative way. Perhaps CENTCOM could explore ways of marrying an SBCT with deep-fire capabilities (either land-based deep-fire units

---

A Sidewise Examination of the Anti-Access Threat Par Excellence: The Impact of Iran's Closing the Strait

To better understand the interplay of geography and anti-access threats, the study team undertook a spreadsheet-based theater-level campaign analysis of the potential impact on campaign outcomes of an Iranian closure of the Strait of Hormuz in a scenario that posited an invasion of southern Iraq, Kuwait, and Saudi Arabia in 2015.

This assessment assumed that Iran would employ a mixed strategy of sea mines, submarines, and antiship missiles to close the strait, which would require MCMs, attack submarines, and reconnaissance and strike assets to clear.

The results of this modeling revealed the importance both of geography as an enabler to anti-access efforts, and the potential—in the limiting condition of geographic advantage—for anti-access strategies to affect campaign outcomes. In this case, Iran's enviable geographic position astride the strait gave it a range of options for delaying movements through the strait, which, in some cases, had discernible impacts both on campaign outcomes, and on the degree to which land forces participated in the campaign.[17]

---

[17] These supporting analyses are available to authorized U.S. government personnel but not to the general public.

or naval or air capabilities) to create stronger forward deterrent ground force packages.

Finally, during an actual conflict with Iraq that involves active Iraqi anti-access efforts, CENTCOM could employ innovative standoff tactics that leverage American deep-fire capabilities (ATACMS, MLRS, Comanche, Apache) to the greatest extent possible and minimize the number of close combat engagements that might result in significant U.S. casualties. These kinds of tactics may call for new types of unit organization in the U.S. Army.

CHAPTER FOUR

The Pacific Theater: A PRC-Taiwan Game

This chapter details our gaming of a PRC-Taiwan scenario. As with the previous chapter, we begin with an overview of the game, summarize our main findings on anti-access threats, and describe the implications regarding access requirements and options available to mitigate regional anti-access strategies.

Overview of the Game

The PRC-Taiwan anti-access scenario explored PRC, U.S., and Taiwanese objectives, strategies, CONOPs, and capabilities in a crisis and conflict scenario in the U.S. Pacific Command (PACOM) area of responsibility in two time frames (2003–2007 and 2012). This scenario was selected as our PACOM regional anti-access case because we believed it to be one of the most stressing long-term conventional contingencies that the United States might plausibly face in the PACOM AOR.[1] It was our "long pole in the tent" for PACOM.

---

[1] In the short term, a North Korean implosion would be stressing as well for PACOM. A contingency pitting the PRC against a unified Korea also would be very stressing in the longer term. This is especially so in light of CIA estimates that Pyongyang may have one or two nuclear weapons and others' belief that North Korea could have even more.

The Scenario

We chose this scenario to help us assess how the Army should think about operating in an anti-access environment where other services have the leading role. Geography in the Taiwan case dictates that U.S. land forces will rely on naval and air forces to do the brunt of the work to neutralize the PRC's preferred anti-access tools. These tools will include attack submarines, advanced sea mines, TBMs, cruise missiles, and SAMs.

The Taiwan scenario placed more of a burden on the Air Force and Navy than on the Army because of the requirement to closely guard strategic airlifters and sealift ships traveling across the Western Pacific into Taiwan. The Army capabilities most relevant to a Taiwan contingency were air defense units, MLRS batteries, attack helicopters, and LMSR sealift ships.

The Taiwan case thus afforded the opportunity to explore concepts for integrating "nontraditional" Army force packages (e.g., those made up of air defense, attack helicopter, and precision rocket artillery units) into combined-arms operations that are largely maritime and aerial in nature. Most important, we found that the PRC will be unable to keep the U.S. military out of Taiwan in either the 2003–2007 or 2012 time frame, but it does have an ability to delay the entry of mission-essential U.S. forces.

Army thrust areas suggested by the scenario included forward-basing of key capabilities, "deep-strike" capabilities, development of a common operational picture, interoperable air defenses, and a wider range of mobility alternatives (e.g., high-speed sealift, lighterage).

Actors, Objectives, CONOPs, and Capabilities

PRC Objectives, CONOPs, and Capabilities. Chinese objectives in our scenario all are aimed at weakening Taiwan's resolve and ability to remain a sovereign entity separate from the mainland. Some slight differences exist between the PRC's objectives in the 2003–2007 period, when China is attempting a limited coercion strategy, and the 2012 period, when China tries a conquering strategy.

In the 2003–2007 period, we assume that members of the PRC leadership are striving to influence the Taiwanese leadership to renounce any thought of continuing Taiwan's independence and accept a Hong Kong–style incorporation into the PRC. At the same time, the Chinese leadership is assumed to want to accomplish incorporation seamlessly and at low cost by not inflicting serious damage on Taiwan's economic infrastructure and by minimizing the level of resentment created among the Taiwanese populace. Finally, the Chinese leaders wish to localize any conflict over Taiwan. Thus, horizontal escalation is to be avoided. China's CONOPs in 2003–2007 are based on an air and sea blockade of Taiwan accompanied by a very muted international political reaction. The blockade is designed to strangle Taiwan economically and convince Taipei that resistance to the PRC can only be counterproductive. Selected offensive strikes against important Taiwanese military bases and units will be mounted, but massive attacks that might kill many civilians are to be avoided to prevent the international community from putting its support behind Taiwan out of sympathy.[2]

By 2012, we posited that the PRC would become more aggressive because its military capabilities have improved. At this time, the Chinese attempt a conquering strategy designed to seize part of Taiwan with ground forces, aiming to push Taipei directly into a fast-track framework for unification talks. In the 2012 time frame, China employs a more direct and aggressive CONOP and actively seeks to hit the island's infrastructure with intense air and missile attacks across Taiwan, followed by an assault. The People's Liberation Army (PLA) is directed to seize a lodgment in southwestern Taiwan and use it to force the Taiwanese Army to mass in the open and thus become vulnerable to PRC air and missile attacks. After the Taiwanese Army is significantly damaged in this way, the PRC plans to offer a ceasefire on harsh diplomatic terms.

A critical part of China's strategy in any Taiwan scenario would be to deter the United States from getting involved to support Tai-

---

[2] One of the reviewers of this report suggested that the PRC war plan could instead be a full-scale invasion attempt with blockade as a possible fallback but that the choice of scenario did not seem to affect the results.

wan militarily. The PRC knows that any U.S. military intervention would greatly reduce its chances of success.

The PRC has four main options for deterring U.S. entry, and these can be pursued simultaneously. First, the PRC could emphasize the potential costs to the United States of intervening in support of Taiwan. This could best be done by noting that China possesses strategic nuclear weapons that could devastate at least a few American cities in the event of a major escalation between Washington and Beijing.[3] Second, the PRC could try to decouple America from its regional allies to complicate the basing problem for the U.S. military. Japan, Australia, and the Philippines would be the major targets of Chinese diplomacy in this respect. Third, the PRC could do its best to distract the United States from the Taiwan theater by using allies and proxies to create military distractions for Washington in other parts of the world vital to the United States, such as Southwest Asia. Finally, the Chinese could attempt to increase the cost of the operations by seeking to inflict large-scale casualties, for example, or targeting high-value mobility systems, hoping to thereby deter the United States from intervening, particularly in the 2003–2007 scenario where China has extremely limited aims.

In both the 2003–2007 and 2012 variants of our scenario, we posited that the PRC's overall strategy has two major components: a blockade strategy designed to strangle Taiwan economically and an access-denial strategy that aims to keep U.S. forces out of the region during any conflict. Success in both components is required for the PRC to prevail.

As noted above, the blockade will try to shut down all commercial traffic into and out of Taiwan. Attack submarine and sea mining

---

[3] In this scenario, we assumed that nuclear weapons would not be used, largely because of the U.S. deterrent. If they were used, however, we would expect their principal targets to include ports and airfields in Taiwan and possibly Japan needed for a buildup, and the impact of their use on these targets would almost certainly be to deny the U.S. access to these bases and push U.S. forces to use other, more distant bases. Additionally, while we generally thought it unlikely, it also could result in a strategic-level decision by U.S. policymakers that the situation had escalated in ways that the U.S. commitment might be called into question. In such a circumstance, it cannot be entirely ruled out that the U.S. might decide to halt further deployments or even withdraw.

capabilities are the primary tools in the blockade component because most major commercial cargo and supplies arrive and depart Taiwan by sea. Electronic warfare (EW) may also be used. Strategically positioned attack submarines and the laying of sea mines in Taiwanese harbors would be the linchpin of a Chinese blockade with some guided-missile destroyers (such as the Russian-built *Sovremennyy*-class DDGs) serving in a backup role. Robust naval C2 capabilities, including some satellite communications, would be needed to orchestrate and maintain this blockade.

The access-denial component would be more air-centric in character to counter U.S. reliance on air power as the leading wedge of any intervention on behalf of the Taiwanese. The United States would have to use strategic airlifters (along with some basic air defense and force protection capability) to get the aerial port laydown teams into Taiwan. If the USAF did not enjoy air superiority over the Taiwan Strait, these heavy transport aircraft would not even be allowed to come near Taiwan. Thus, if the People's Liberation Army Air Force (PLAAF) were able to prevent or delay the establishment of U.S. air superiority over the Taiwan Strait, it would have largely achieved China's anti-access objectives. Because the PLAAF's pilots and tactical fighter aircraft are not the equal of those of the USAF and USN, Chinese air superiority denial efforts will likely center on advanced air defense systems (especially Russian-manufactured "double-digit" SAMs) and TBM attacks on major Taiwanese air bases that would host such U.S. airlift aircraft as the C-17 and C-5.

The major PRC capabilities include attack submarines and sea mining capabilities, with surface combatants in a backup role, conducting the naval blockade and aiming to force U.S. naval assets to operate at greater distances. They also include air and ballistic missile capabilities (and by 2012, perhaps cruise missiles as well), which are used to attack leadership, C2, population, and access-related infrastructure targets, and assault forces to seize and hold a lodgment on Taiwan. Extended-range SAMs and SOF teams with man-portable air defense systems are used to harass U.S. airlifters and other U.S. and Taiwanese aircraft.

U.S. Objectives, CONOPs, and Capabilities. In our two scenarios, the United States has largely similar objectives. In 2012, one new objective has been added because of China's employment of a conquer strategy in that time frame.

Like China, the United States desires to confine any combat to Taiwan and the Taiwan Strait. This is because any escalation to a wider war would risk a strategic nuclear exchange between China and the United States. Beyond that, U.S. objectives are obvious. Taiwan's airports and seaports need to be protected from air and missile strikes, and Chinese threats to air and sea traffic have to be negated. In short, the United States seeks to crack the PRC blockade of Taiwan and push the issue of Taiwan back on a purely diplomatic track. In 2012, the United States also seeks to repulse Chinese assault forces working to establish a lodgment in southeastern Taiwan.

The U.S. CONOP for the defense of Taiwan is straightforward. In the first phase, it is imperative that the USAF and USN achieve air superiority over the Taiwan Strait in concert with Taiwan's Air Force. Simultaneously, the United States will have to conduct a naval campaign to destroy most of the PRC's attack submarines and surface ships in the vicinity of Taiwan. The second phase of the U.S. CONOP will entail the opening of major ports with minesweeping vessels and the aerial flow of air and missile defense units (e.g., Patriot batteries) into Taiwan early in the deployment to guard major air bases. The third phase would conclude the CONOP with the provision of direct logistical support to Taiwan in the form of oil, food, and medicine.

In the 2003–2007 case, U.S. forces employed would be heavily naval in character. Aircraft carrier battle groups (including nuclear attack submarines [SSNs]) and minesweepers would be used to gain air superiority, break the PRC blockade, and open major ports. Land-based tactical air would play a role in helping to gain air superiority as well. Substantial sealift and airlift assets would be deployed to both resupply Taiwan's economy and bring in some limited missile defense units.

In the 2012 case, a fourth phase would be added in which selected U.S. Army capabilities, like attack helicopters and MLRS/

ATACMS, would be introduced to help repel the PRC's amphibious invasion or eliminate the PRC's lodgment on Taiwan.[4] The 2012 case would include significant ground forces as well because of the limited Chinese ground invasion. Theater missile defense (TMD) batteries (Patriot and THAAD) for the protection of key APODs and attack helicopters and rocket artillery for attacks on incoming Chinese amphibious vessels would be added to the naval and air packages. Additionally in 2012, because of the more aggressive CONOP, the United States would probably consider using heavy bombers, such as the B-2, to strike selected C2 and IADS targets on the Chinese mainland itself. It goes without saying that these targets must be picked carefully to avoid an undesired escalation.

Taiwanese Objectives, CONOPs, and Capabilities. Taiwan's presumed objectives, CONOP, and forces in our scenario show that Taiwan's military is highly capable in certain areas and its assistance will be critical to any American effort to counter anti-access measures.

In general, Taiwan's objectives closely resemble those of the United States. Taipei also wants to defend its sovereignty, protect the island from air and missile strikes, and remove threats to incoming air and shipping traffic. The two objectives that are unique to Taiwan are the encouragement of maximum U.S. involvement and the management of world opinion to favor Taiwan and swing against the PRC. In the area of CONOPs, the goals and tasks of Taiwan are also largely congruent with the U.S. military's. Indeed, the two sides would probably agree on a common CONOP even before actual hostilities commence. However, two aspects of the CONOP remain unique to Taiwan because of the specifically Taiwanese objectives mentioned above. First, the Taiwanese regime would seek to preserve as many of its valuable military assets as possible (fighter aircraft, warships) to retain a powerful military at the conclusion of hostilities that could increase its leverage with the PRC in postwar negotiations. Second, in the event of an actual PRC ground invasion in the 2012

---

[4] Obviously, a key assumption of this is the likelihood that U.S. policymakers would make a decision to employ ground forces. We included this phase to explore the question of what land forces could be employed in such a scenario.

time frame, the Taiwanese would seek to maximize the involvement of U.S. ground forces in the island's defense.

Taiwan's military is well trained and highly professional. However, gaps in Taiwan's capabilities exist that the PRC could exploit if U.S. support to the island is not forthcoming.

Taiwan's Air Force has three times more fourth-generation fighters (including F-16s) than does the PRC and its pilot quality is definitely superior as well. However, the latest official DoD report on Chinese military power indicates that Chinese pilot training is steadily improving and Taiwanese pilots seem to be "overworked." Although Taiwan has fairly modern surveillance, battle management, and C2 aircraft, it lacks dependable theater missile defenses and may not have adequate civil defense measures in place to protect its populace from terror attacks with SRBMs. Taiwan's surface navy has a sprinkling of modern destroyers, frigates, and fast attack craft, but its diesel submarine fleet is antiquated and offers little in the way of combat power against the growing Chinese submarine fleet.

By 2012, the Taiwanese may be able to improve their overall naval capability through the addition of more dedicated minesweepers, the purchase of destroyers with Aegis radar from the United States, and the acquisition of a few modern diesel-electric submarines. Absent these modernization moves, the PRC's ability to execute a naval blockade will improve by 2012.

Findings

Overall, we judged that the Chinese military as it is currently configured poses a manageable set of anti-access threats to American forces. However, it should be mentioned that the PRC has more anti-access options and greater quantities of anti-access tools than Saddam Hussein's Iraq had.

Moreover, the upshot of this analysis is that, if current trends continue, PRC anti-access capabilities will improve both qualitatively and quantitatively over the next decade. Barring a more rapid pace in U.S. naval, stealth attack, and theater missile defense research and development spending, it appears as if the anti-access challenge for the United States in a Taiwan scenario will be more difficult in 2012 than it is today.

Key Access Issues

In-Theater. In terms of the deployment route itself, the most vulnerable nodes overall were in the theater of operation—the Taiwanese APODs and SPODs. This was principally because of their location within range of China's CSS-6 and CSS-7 TBMs.

Only a limited number of air bases are suitable for U.S. transport aircraft on the southern half of the island. Furthermore, only two ports on the eastern coast of Taiwan have the depth necessary to dock U.S. LMSR sealift ships—the vessels that would be used to bring significant Army forces into the Western Pacific. The small number of suitable APODs and SPODs means that a successful PRC missile strike on any one node would cause major disruptions and delays to the U.S. deployment timetable.

Enough potential APODs on Taiwan and a sufficiently robust en-route infrastructure make it unlikely that a Chinese anti-access strategy based on airfield denial would succeed, however. Even with 75 percent of the preferred APODs on Taiwan destroyed, sufficient theoretical throughput would allow for timely closure of a TBM Defense Task Force, consisting of Patriot PAC-3 Brigade and robust force protection capabilities.[5] In addition, in the unlikely event that Japanese airports were denied to U.S. aircraft, other en-route bases are sufficient for this scenario.[6] However, the deployment of additional AMC personnel and equipment, either in peacetime or during

---

[5] Our notion for force protection was a light infantry battalion, an assault aviation company task force, an air defense artillery battalion, and engineering and forward support units.

[6] Other states in the region offer possible en-route bases for U.S. airlift aircraft as well. In all cases, however, these are less desirable than their counterparts in Japan, South Korea, Guam, and Hawaii because of geographic position relative to Taiwan. Australia, the Philippines, Brunei, Cambodia, Laos, the Northern Marianas, Micronesia, Palau, and Papua New Guinea all contain possible en-route bases for AMC aircraft. Bases in the Philippines, while not optimal for airlift operations in a Taiwan contingency, would be well suited as secondary operating locations for U.S. tactical fighter units during any Taiwan contingency.

a crisis, likely could easily overcome the basing constraints resulting from destruction or denial of the preferred APODs.

En Route. En-route vulnerabilities were judged to be minor overall. The United States has a substantial en-route infrastructure in the Western Pacific that is unlikely to face the threat of serious damage from the Chinese military. In the en-route infrastructure, Yokota Air Base (AB) on the Japanese island of Honshu was identified as an important transit point in the Pacific. Any degradation of Yokota's throughput would be only a minor negative for U.S. mobility planners, however, because Japan has a rich air base infrastructure with many alternate bases. The PRC's ability to precisely target Yokota with long-range systems, while weak now, could improve if they chose to pursue such capabilities. If, on the other hand, PRC political pressure persuaded Japanese leaders to deny access to its bases for all U.S. forces involved in the defense of Taiwan, some modest negative repercussions for the U.S. mobility strategy would result because U.S. airlift forces would then be required to take the more circuitous southern route across the Central Pacific.

Finally, one wild card in the U.S. deployment network is the Panama Canal. The canal would be used to move LMSR sealift vessels into the Pacific because all LMSRs are currently home-ported on the East Coast. If one or two Chinese SSNs positioned themselves at the Pacific end of the canal and attacked LMSRs exiting the canal, the results for the U.S. deployment CONOP in this Taiwan scenario would be grim indeed. However, the likelihood of the PRC being able to deploy two SSNs over such a long range is rated as low, and the U.S. Navy's antisubmarine warfare (ASW) capabilities are, in any case, quite robust against such a threat.[7]

CONUS. China's ability to take any anti-access campaign to the U.S. homeland is quite limited and likely to remain so, even into the 2012 time frame. Of the five potential mechanisms for attacking CONUS to disrupt an U.S. deployment to Taiwan, three (computer

---

[7] Our study was fortunate to have, as a member of the study team, a Navy submariner who was exceedingly knowledgeable about ASW capabilities.

network attacks, IO and PSYOPS, SOF and irregular forces attacks) are rated as posing only tertiary-level threats in both time frames while two (ICBM threats and CBRNE attacks) were scored as wild cards dependent on several external variables.

Threats of Greatest Concern

China has only a limited number of other tools with which to try to prevent the deployment of U.S. ground forces to Taiwan. However, the Chinese military would attempt to delay and disrupt the U.S. deployment by deploying these tools in a complementary fashion.

Advanced Sea Mines and Attack Submarines. Mining of ports was rated as the most dangerous overall because it was seen as a serious threat in both 2003–2007 and 2012. China has purchased significant numbers of very advanced mines on the world market and could conceivably deploy them covertly in significant numbers even before the official commencement of hostilities. This could be done from merchant trawlers or diesel attack submarines. Any Chinese employment of submarines could well be two-pronged in approach. *Kilo*-model diesel submarines would be used to directly guard the entrances to the main SPODs while longer-endurance nuclear attack submarines of the Type 093 class (which has not yet been deployed) could form a cordon at a distance of about 200–300 nautical miles east of the Taiwanese coast. Both kinds of submarines would probably be equipped with sophisticated wake homing torpedoes. Compounding the situation is the fact that U.S. Navy warships today have poor organic minesweeping capabilities and few MCM assets deployed in the Pacific theater.

A related anti-access option for the Chinese would be to construct a maritime barrier of advanced sea mines and attack submarines to try to prevent American military cargo ships from entering the large Taiwanese SPODs. Such a barrier also raises the possibility that the Chinese might be able to sink a U.S. LMSR sealift ship containing large amounts of valuable equipment, thus significantly delaying the establishment of a strong U.S. attack helicopter presence on Taiwan.

TBM Attacks on APODs/SPODs. The PRC has a growing arsenal of CSS-6 and CSS-7 SRBMs deployed on the southern Chinese coast opposite Taiwan. Some estimates indicate that the total could exceed 650 by the middle of this decade. Because the PLAAF currently has only a few advanced fourth-generation fighter-bombers in its inventory and also faces a paucity of well-trained fighter pilots, SRBMs are, at least over the near term, the PRC's main instrument for long-range strikes against key ports and airfields on Taiwan. In the 2012 time frame, a real possibility exists that the Chinese may have one or two long-range land attack cruise missile (LACM) systems to complement SRBMs as an offensive strike tool against Taiwanese APODs and SPODs. The accuracy of PRC missiles also may improve (e.g., as a result of integrating GPS guidance capabilities), as could the C3ISR capabilities needed to exploit this additional accuracy.

If the Chinese employ their SRBM force as a dedicated anti-access tool, as opposed to a pure psychological warfare instrument, they would need to either use massed barrage attacks against a few specific APODs and SPODs or use a small number of SRBMs equipped with chemical warheads that could contaminate air bases and ports with persistent blistering or nerve agents. Although neither approach is guaranteed to succeed, to the extent that U.S. commanders essentially write off bases that have been attacked with such weapons, their effects could be significant. Of course, the use of nuclear-tipped missiles would have much more significant impact on APODs or SPODs, in may cases completely destroying them. Although we generally assumed that nuclear weapons would not be used, if they were used, they could greatly change the situation.

Ballistic missiles or cruise missiles with submunitions would be especially valuable in that they could crater runways or taxiways on these bases or destroy aircraft and scarce material-handling equipment (MHE). SRBMs would likely be used to disrupt operations at major Taiwanese air bases and ports. This would have the effect of both lowering the operations tempo of the well-trained and equipped Taiwanese Air Force and making it more difficult for U.S. strategic lift assets to flow into Taiwan. With luck, the PRC might even fire one of its SRBMs at a time when it would destroy a U.S. airlift aircraft or some key MHE assets on the tarmac.

Analysis done to support this report indicates that it would take 25–50 missiles with a 300-meter CEP to close a single runway with 90 percent probability;[8] cruise missiles or more accurate ballistic missiles could do much better. If one follows this path of reasoning, most of China's current SRBM force would be exhausted in an effort to close down—albeit temporarily (i.e., until they can be repaired)—just six runways with a high probability. If air and missile defense capabilities can be made effective, the salvo requirements are even larger. Use of chemical warheads is risky also because a combination of poor meteorological conditions and the use of basic protective gear and gross decontamination of personnel and equipment by Taiwanese and U.S. personnel could largely nullify a chemical missile attack on APODs and SPODs. The introduction of effective area-denial warheads, including runway penetrators, could lower the number of missiles required to close an airfield.

The team assumed that, if China has an inventory of 650 SRBMs, they would need to reserve perhaps 30–40 percent of their missile stock to have a high probability of destroying an undefended LMSR. Such a commitment would limit China to between 15 and 19 missile strikes a day during the first 25 days of the campaign. Thus while an LMSR is a high-value target, Chinese strategic opportunity costs would be high in terms of coercive political and economic targets left unharmed. Compounding this problem for China is their lack of specific knowledge of when, or even if, an LMSR would arrive.[9] Other port facilities are either relatively robust or difficult to target with SRBMs. Simply putting craters in a berth or its environs is unlikely to impede U.S. offloading operations significantly. Unless the crater is precisely positioned to block the unloading of equipment

---

[8] This is a nearer-term case, as it seems likely that the accuracy of ballistic missiles will improve given access to GPS and GLONASS.

[9] We do, however, acknowledge the possibility that the PRC might be able to acquire near real-time imagery or human intelligence that could assist in determining LMSR arrival schedules.

from the LMSR it can easily be avoided. In addition, repair requirements for such craters are unlikely to be as stringent as those of an
airfield runway. Such critical equipment as ramps and cranes are
relatively small and thus would require an even greater expenditure of
inaccurate SRBMs if they are to be successfully destroyed. While a
warhead with submunitions would have a greater chance of hitting a
berth or an LMSR, the damage it would cause is likely to be relatively
superficial. Such a warhead, however, could be extremely effective
against exposed materiel and personnel. As a result, a premium would
be put on rapidly dispersing offloaded equipment from the LMSR.

The bottom line is that even though an LMSR is a high-value
target from the perspective of U.S. deployment, China is unlikely to
reserve the missiles necessary to sink one unless it is convinced that
such a result would have a significant strategic, rather then tactical,
effect on the overall campaign.

Creation of a SAM Umbrella over Parts of Taiwan. In addition to its ballistic missiles, a second option for the PLA would be to
block the aerial approaches to Taiwan's major APODs and SPODs
by establishing a SAM umbrella that covers much of the northern
half of the island, increasing the risk to airlifters and perhaps even
forcing them to fly circuitous routes to get to the main APODs on
the east coast of Taiwan (especially if they are flying south from
Japan). Such a SAM umbrella would not only be a valuable anti-
access tool for the Chinese, it also could be a part of their strategy to
prevent the U.S. and Taiwanese Air Forces from achieving outright
air superiority over the Taiwan Strait.

The establishment of this kind of umbrella would require significant numbers of long-range double-digit Russian manufactured
SAMs, such as the SA-10 and S-400. Furthermore, these missiles
would need to either be fitted with active terminal seekers or have the
ability to accept targeting information and updates from airborne
platforms to locate and destroy airlifters with flight profiles below the
radar horizon of targeting radars on the Chinese mainland. It also
could require a very sophisticated integrated air defense C2 network,

some pieces of which would need to be placed on relatively vulnerable aerial platforms.[10] China has neither right now, but if Russia continues its willingness to sell the PRC large quantities of its best air defense technology in the next several years, such a SAM umbrella might be a possibility in the 2010–2015 time frame.[11] Thus, a strong possibility exists that the advanced SAM threat could present a much more serious anti-access threat in the future.

Strike Aircraft and Land Attack Cruise Missiles. In addition to using ballistic missiles, China would selectively use its fourth-generation fighter aircraft (Su-27, Su-30MK) to strike at critical Taiwanese port facilities, military air traffic C2 nodes, and U.S. sealift ships at berth in the local SPODs with standoff precision-guided munitions.[12] If, over time, PLAAF pilot training and aircraft maintenance capability improve, the role of manned attack aircraft in China's anti-access strategy for Taiwan will likely grow in importance. However, in the near-term future, fighter aircraft will remain a secondary tool in the PRC's anti-access approach. LACMs were not rated at all for 2003–2007 because the PRC does not yet have operational LACMs. By 2012, however, they should be in the PLA inventory and would represent a growing threat.

Other Threats Considered

CBRNE WMD. Both the Chinese ICBM force and China's capability to mount CBRNE attacks were rated as wild cards for 2003–2007 and 2012 because the nature of both threats to the United States is highly context-dependent. The level of the PRC's ICBM threat will depend, for example, on the progress the United States has made toward deploying an effective nuclear missile defense system and on

---

[10] One of our reviewers suggested that the threat to airlifters could be significant even without such a network.

[11] The PRC currently is developing a SAM that should be equivalent to the SA-10 called the HQ-9.

[12] David A. Shlapak, David T. Orletsky, and Barry Wilson, *Dire Strait? Military Aspects of the China-Taiwan Confrontation and Options for U.S. Policy*, Santa Monica, Calif.: RAND Corporation, MR-1217-SRF, 2000.

the size of the PRC ICBM force at the time of a confrontation, but a robust nuclear missile defense capability seems unlikely by 2012.[13] The risk of CBRNE attacks instigated by the PRC will, on the other hand, be determined by such factors as whether the PRC develops SOF capabilities to employ CBRNE or forms partnerships with international terrorist groups and by the willingness of Chinese leaders to supply such groups with usable WMD or attempt to introduce such weapons covertly (e.g., in a container on a ship or by a small aircraft).

PSYOPS and IO. Team members did not believe that China could achieve enough of an advantage over the United States in the areas of IW or PSYOPS to use these methods to slow down a U.S. military response to a Taiwan crisis. Information security for key DoD systems is improving and, as better encryption software is developed and put into place, it will only become better. Also, China's offensive IW capabilities, while certainly significant, are not generally thought of as among the best in the world. Russia, for example, likely has a more advanced offensive IW portfolio.

SOF. Another potential anti-access tool that the PRC could use, at least on the psychological level, would be small SOF teams inserted into Taiwan to target U.S. airlifters with man-portable air defense systems. Even if only one transport were downed as a result, the effect would likely be a halt in airlift operations until Taiwanese security forces could exhaustively sweep all areas adjacent to major air bases. SOF also might use mortars, rocket-propelled grenades, remotely detonated explosive devices, or a variety of other means to threaten airlift (or sealift) or hinder movement from APODs and SPODs.

Implications for Regional Commanders

An active security cooperation plan was viewed by our team as critical to building the types of political relationships with East Asian states

---

[13] "DIA (Defense Intelligence Agency) Testimony," 2002.

that would deter Chinese leaders from attempting offensive action against Taiwan in the first place. As part of the theater engagement, we recommend that the Army consider forward basing of assets that would be needed to protect Taiwan in the event of war. Either Taiwan should ensure the adequacy of air defense capabilities or these assets should be positioned on the U.S. West Coast, Hawaii, and Guam or the Northern Marianas.

Access Requirements

In the Taiwan scenario, the requirements for the commander of PACOM to achieve full access to the region are straightforward and clearly defined: the principal focus of the PACOM commander, PACOM access efforts ought to be protecting the key APODs and SPODs in Taiwan and ensuring that the immediate approaches to these facilities remain unobstructed by PRC forces.[14]

Protecting the Key APODs and SPODs in Taiwan. The main Taiwanese APODs and SPODs must be kept operational even when they are under attack by missiles and ballistic missiles and/or advanced fighter bombers. This means that Chinese long-range SAMs cannot be allowed to form a "coverage umbrella" that blocks the air corridors U.S. airlifters must transit to land at the main Taiwanese APODs. In addition, the access requirements in this Taiwan scenario make it imperative that the main east and south coast SPODs do not have their entrances blocked by either sea mines or attack submarines.

The PACOM commander can afford to focus on the security of Taiwanese APODs and SPODs because the en-route infrastructure that would be used to move U.S. forces to Taiwan in a crisis or conflict has significant redundancy. Thus, it would not be overly burdened by the quantity of forces required for deployment in this scenario. Perhaps even more important, the Chinese military does

---

[14] Our project team made the assessment that the most important APODs on Taiwan for this scenario are Hualien, Fengnin, Pingtung South, and Kaohsiung. SPODs of primary importance are Hualien and Kaohsiung. Most of these facilities are on the east or south sides of Taiwan, where they are less vulnerable to attack by ballistic missiles and tactical combat aircraft.

not, at least in the near term, have the kind of long-range precision-strike systems that would be needed to have a good chance of successfully targeting parts of the U.S. en-route basing infrastructure in the Western Pacific. By the 2012 time frame, the Chinese may have developed a class of nuclear attack submarines (Type 093) or IRBMs that could threaten American forces moving through Northeast Asia or the Marianas.

Requirements of Allies. The only indispensable ally in this scenario would be Taiwan itself. It is absolutely imperative that the Taiwanese Air Force and Navy avoid heavy, debilitating losses in the opening days of a PRC attack so that the United States can swing the balance of the conflict against the PRC with only a modest commitment of combat forces to Taiwan itself.[15] If the Taiwanese take unnecessary risks with their advanced fighter aircraft and naval combatant vessels early in a Chinese attack, the United States may be forced to deploy relatively large amounts of combat power to Taiwan (including significant ground forces), which would greatly complicate the anti-access problem for the commander of PACOM.

Other allies and partners in the Western Pacific could be helpful to the U.S. effort, but they would not be indispensable. Japan and South Korea could provide a great service by allowing AMC aircraft to use some of their main air bases as intermediate staging bases in the deployment chain from CONUS to Taiwan. Japan also could ease the U.S. burden in this scenario by allowing U.S. tactical fighter aircraft, intelligence, surveillance, and reconnaissance (ISR) aircraft, and tankers to operate from Kadena AB on Okinawa, which is only slightly more than 100 nautical miles from Taiwan. Access to Kadena could obviate the need for the United States to place land-based tactical air units on Taiwan itself. However, as noted earlier, if the Japanese and South Koreans denied access to the United States, AMC could still gain access to Taiwan by building a deployment chain across the Central Pacific. In such a circumstance, AMC would need

---

[15] The ability of the United States to influence the outcome with only a modest commitment of forces may become increasingly difficult, however, if the PRC continues to build its military capabilities at the current pace and if Taiwan fails to keep up.

longer-range, land-based combat aircraft or heavier reliance on in-theater bases. The Philippines could likewise aid the U.S. effort by providing access to tactical fighter bases on the northern island of Luzon. American aircraft carriers might also be able to dock at the old Subic Bay port for rest and refit during any Taiwan contingency.

Options for the PACOM Commander

Peacetime. In peacetime, the commander of PACOM can improve the chances for American success in our Taiwan scenario by engaging with potential American allies and partners, posturing U.S. forces forward in the Pacific, and encouraging the Taiwanese to make serious efforts to harden and otherwise improve their defenses—particularly airfields—against Chinese missile attacks.

Maintaining strong political-military and military-to-military relations with Japan during peacetime would increase the chances that Japan would be receptive to American requests for base access during a Taiwan scenario. Continued expansion of cooperation with the Philippines also could improve the chances that it would grant the U.S. access to its bases during any China-Taiwan confrontation.

Currently, most of the assets that would have to be deployed to Taiwan in our scenario (attack helicopters, LMSRs, etc.) are home based in the eastern half of CONUS. By allowing some of these assets be home based on the U.S. West Coast, in Hawaii, or perhaps even in Guam or the Northern Marianas, the United States would increase the number of flexible deterrent options that would be available during any crisis with the PRC over Taiwan.

Finally, the PACOM commander could increase the time line in which U.S. forces can safely deploy to Taiwan by encouraging the Taiwanese to harden their island more than it has been in the past. This would include the enactment of an extensive nationwide civil defense program, the procurement of more minesweeping ships, additional shelters and revetments for airfields, burying key C2 facilities, and acquiring more chemical and biological warfare decontamination equipment. It also would encourage the development of more robust air and missile defenses.[16]

Crisis. In a crisis, measures that could be taken by PACOM could include the timely initiation of flexible deterrence options that would draw on equipment forward-deployed in the Pacific region in peacetime. For example, a few anti-TBM batteries could be deployed into Taiwan in a crisis, and one or two aircraft carriers could be moved into the waters off Taiwan. Efforts to demonstrate that the United States would quickly win information superiority in any war over Taiwan also could be helpful in deterring computer network attacks and other offensive information operations. Preliminary EW and IW probes of key PRC C2 systems could be helpful in this regard, as would capabilities to credibly threaten Chinese reconnaissance and imaging satellites—e.g., through jamming of sensors or communications lines, attacking ground-based facilities, or establishing a ground-based antisatellite system somewhere in the Central Pacific that could threaten the satellites.

Conflict. In a conflict, the most innovative ideas that came out of this game involved the formation of ground-based deep-strike packages and formations that could target both an amphibious assault and Chinese SRBM launchers and SAM sites from their positions on Taiwan. It remains to be demonstrated whether such a capability actually is needed in light of current and planned sea-based and air-based capabilities for deep attack. Team members repeatedly discussed the importance of forming a dedicated deep-strike task force that would train together in peacetime and be capable of conducting counteramphibious assault operations and counterbattery operations against Chinese SAM and conventional TBM launchers.[17] Counterbattery operations against nuclear missile launchers would, of course,

---

[16] Of course, cost-effectiveness considerations may suggest that such efforts should await the development of a new generation of more effective TMD systems.

[17] Current counterbattery capabilities may lack the necessary range. The Army may wish to explore options that would provide additional deep-fire capabilities for counterbattery operations against launchers for conventional missiles—e.g., using ATACMS, the High-Mobility Artillery Rocket System, attack helicopters, SOF, or other options.

risk launch on attack and a dramatic escalation of the conflict past the nuclear threshold. In any event, such a task force would likely consist of a mix of MLRS/ATACMS batteries and, possibly, attack helicopters.[18] The strike team also might acquire its own organic UAVs and links to data provided from national overhead assets. An analysis of the military effectiveness, cost-effectiveness, and robustness of such a concept might help establish the conditions under which such a package might be superior to other operational concepts (e.g., those that emphasize aerial delivery platforms).

Lashing up the Army's digital battlefield to a joint and combined information grid to provide a common operational picture also would help improve combat effectiveness.[19] The existence of a common operational picture also would help ground-based anti-TBMs to work seamlessly with air- and sea-based anti-TBM systems.

Finally, we believe that combat performance in our Taiwan scenario could be improved through the development of regionally based joint IW force packages that would have many East Asian linguists and intelligence analysts in its ranks. This package would include SOF and IW units and would work to conduct strategic reconnaissance, PSYOPS, computer network attack, EW, and deception operations throughout the theater.

---

[18] The team also recognized that counterbattery attacks could constitute an important escalatory step and that considerable thought would need to be given to employment of such a capability.

[19] The "battlespace infosphere" is one name given to the concept for a joint system-of-systems architecture that can provide persistent, real-time, comprehensive situational assessment data and a common operational picture. The concept is most closely identified with retired General James P. McCarthy and is elaborated in his June 12, 2002 special news briefing on defense transformation, the transcript of which is available at http://www.defenselink.mil.

CHAPTER FIVE

European Theater: A Russia-Baltics Game

This chapter details our gaming of a Russia-Baltics scenario. As we did in the previous chapters, we begin with an overview of the game and then summarize our findings, detail the implications for access requirements, and describe options available to reduce the efficacy of regional anti-access strategies.

Overview of the Game

The Baltics anti-access scenario explored Russian, U.S., NATO, and Baltic states objectives, strategies, CONOPs, and capabilities in an invasion scenario in the U.S. European Command (EUCOM) area of responsibility in two time frames (2003–2007 and 2012). The scenario involved a Russian attempt to employ military coercion to separate the three Baltic states (Lithuania, Latvia, and Estonia) from NATO.

The Scenario
The Baltic scenario was useful because it allowed for an exploration of anti-access issues in a region where much of the strategic movement into the theater of operations would occur over land routes and where the opponent was armed with small quantities of indigenously produced advanced weaponry.

The general background for this scenario was a deteriorating U.S.-Russian relationship.[1] The continued expansion of NATO to Russia's border in northern and eastern Europe and the continued presence of U.S. bases in Central Asia, an area traditionally within the Russian sphere of interest, led Russia to feel increasingly encircled and vulnerable. This perception was reinforced by Russia's obvious conventional military weakness and by the belief that U.S. nuclear missile defense deployments would deny Russia a secure second-strike capability. Feeling increasingly threatened and vulnerable, Russia's political and military elites were in no mood to passively accept that NATO's enlargement into the Baltic states is an irreversible act. The United States, for its part, was angered by continued Russian close ties with Iran and came increasingly to view Russia as an enabler of the "axis of evil" rather than as a reliable or responsible global partner. This perception left U.S. political elites in no mood to accommodate Russian fears and delay or prevent the voluntary entry of three demo-cratic states into NATO. With neither state willing or able to com-promise, the potential for a conflict in the Baltic region grew.

The catalyst for the crisis in the Baltic states was the failure of Estonia and Latvia to fully integrate their ethnic Russian populations by completing the process of granting them full citizenship rights and by ending discriminatory practices. This continued discriminatory treatment fostered resentment among the region's ethnic Russian populations, causing them to become increasingly hostile towards their governments, to begin a protest campaign for increased civil rights, and to look toward Russia for support. This environment allowed the Russian intelligence services to exploit existing protests

---

[1] It is important to note that in developing this scenario the anti-access team assumed that, because both the United States and Russia had robust nuclear arsenals and because both wished to avoid a wider conflict, there would be significant restraints on their respective actions. As a result it was assumed that, at least initially, Russia would not seek to systemati-cally attack targets in CONUS or Western Europe and that NATO would refrain from striking targets throughout Russia. In addition, NATO was assumed to be constrained by Russia's publicly stated doctrine of resorting to tactical and theater nuclear weapons both to defend its national territory and to prevent a significant military defeat. Similarly, it was also assumed that Russia would refrain from utilizing chemical or biological weapons as an anti-access tool out of fear that the use of such weapons would dangerously escalate the conflict.

and unrest by providing financing and organizational expertise to increase the effectiveness, level, and intensity of ethnic Russian protest activities. As the crisis intensified, ethnic Russian extremists attacked government installations and provoked a violent crackdown by regional state security forces. This crackdown, in turn, provided Russia with an opportunity to present itself as a protector of human rights and by doing so attempt to drive a wedge between the Baltic states and their NATO allies.

NATO, however, reacts strongly to Russia's threats against its three newest members, demands a cessation to Russian provocative actions, and begins to take military measures to provide for the defense of the Baltic states. This strong and unanticipated NATO reaction provokes a domestic crisis within the Russian government. Fearing that the loss of both international and domestic face will lead to a collapse of the government, the Russian leadership orders an invasion of the Baltic states as soon as the Russian military can be mobilized and deployed. The Russian military believes that this will take 30 days and that no provocative actions must be taken during this period because the only chance of a Russian success, slim as that might be, depends on the ability to strike first when it is fully mobilized and to thus present NATO with a fait accompli that will lead to a negotiated settlement acceptable to Russia.

The scenario assumed that Russia and Belarus successfully completed their plans to integrate their air defense systems and that their efforts toward political and economic integration were sufficiently advanced that Belarus will be willing to provide at least limited support for Russia in a confrontation with NATO over the Baltic states. This support would be limited to the use of the joint air defense system.

U.S. deployment operations benefited greatly from the low levels of Russian military readiness. The necessity for Russian forces to undergo a lengthy mobilization process of at least 30 days provided the United States with a degree of strategic warning that could be used to make deployment decisions and to begin the lengthy process of building up forces in the region. Furthermore, Russia's requirement for an unimpeded mobilization period gave NATO a distinct asymmetric advantage. Because Russia required a lengthy mobilization period, it was deterred from militarily interfering with NATO's deployment process by attacking strategic lift assets, mining harbors, or striking at ports and airfields, lest NATO respond in kind and precipitate a conflict before the Russian military was ready.

Actors, Objectives, CONOPs, and Capabilities

Russian Objectives, CONOPs, and Capabilities. Russia's primary peacetime theater objectives are to improve the quality of its forces in the St. Petersburg Military District in preparation for possible military contingencies and to try to separate the Baltic states from NATO by nonmilitary means. During conflict, Russia's overarching crisis objective is the "Finlandization" of the Baltic states to remove them from NATO and to thereby eliminate a perceived potential threat to Russia's northern flank by restoring a buffer zone between Russia and NATO. Equally important, Russia wants to avoid a vertical escalation of the crisis because this could threaten the ultimate survival of both the Russian state and the Russian nation. Russia also wants to limit NATO's military access to the Baltic states during the operation to prevent the establishment of NATO bridgeheads, particularly in strategic regions, that would strengthen NATO's postwar position.

The Russian CONOP has four basic themes. The first is that the Russian military needs at least 30 days to mobilize if it is to have a chance of successfully achieving its strategic goals. As a result, no offensive anti-access operations can be conducted during this period. The second is to isolate the Baltic states to prevent the timely introduction of NATO forces. The third is to rapidly overrun the Baltic States so as to present NATO with a fait accompli and strengthen the Russian position in postconflict negotiations. The fourth theme is to prepare to repel a NATO counterattack should it become necessary to do so. Russian airborne troops will seize and hold a series of coastal enclaves as well as the capitals of Latvia and Estonia. These initial lodgments are to be rapidly reinforced by heavy forces moving westward and southward from the St. Petersburg Military District. Mobile SAM systems will accompany these troops and create an IADS over the Baltic states.

Simultaneously with these operations, Russian forces in the Kaliningrad enclave will attempt to seal the Polish-Lithuanian border to prevent the timely intervention of NATO heavy forces that are massing in eastern Poland. This operation is to be assisted by Russian long-range fires, tactical air strikes, and SOF troops who will attempt to destroy railheads, NATO forward cantonments, and key bridges in Poland to blunt the NATO counteroffensive before it can begin. Once these operations have been completed, the Russian military will dig in to repel the NATO counterattack and await a negotiated settlement of the crisis.

The bulk of Russian ground forces consists of two airborne divisions, three motorized rifle divisions, two tank divisions, a *Spetznaz* brigade used to seize vital airfields and chokepoints, and three battalions of TBMs; most of these ground forces came from the St. Petersburg Military District, which is one of the best resourced in Russia. About 200 tactical combat aircraft and 100 bombers, 50 attack helicopters, and other support aircraft are also posited in the scenario. Also important are Russian naval capabilities, such as diesel attack submarines and aircraft with long-range antiship missiles, which are used to prevent NATO maritime access to the Baltic Sea. Russia's integrated air defense network of long-range double-digit SAMs restrict NATO's ability to use airpower to slow the advance of the Russian Army.

In our scenario, Russia's military capability still suffers from the long period of neglect experienced during the 1990s and into the twenty-first century, during which the Russian military could not procure new weapons systems, maintain and operate those it already possessed, or adequately train the personnel required to use them effectively in combat. In this scenario we posit a limited Russian military "renaissance" starting in about 2005–2006, too late to allow for the correction of more than 15 years of neglect by 2007 and the effects of which, if sustained, would likely only begin to become apparent by 2012. Given a still-limited procurement budget, the Russian military focuses on purchasing "silver bullet" weapon systems, such as advanced attack submarines and advanced fourth-generation fighter aircraft that can have a large effect even if present in only small numbers.[2] The Russian military also focuses on the training and maintaining of a small cadre of elite units, accepting the risks involved in letting the readiness and capabilities of the rest of the active military decay significantly.

U.S. Objectives, CONOPs, and Capabilities. The primary U.S. theater objective is to continue expanding and consolidating American and NATO military influence into the Baltic region while restraining Russia's efforts to maintain and reestablish its regional dominance. The United States will also seek to continue the institutionalization of democratic principles in the Baltic states. An important result of this effort would be to decrease the discrimination against ethnic Russians and thus remove one potential motive for Russian interference in the region. In addition, continuing efforts will be made to complete the full integration of the small Baltic militaries into NATO and to finish bringing them up to NATO standards in such selected areas as MCM and air traffic control.[3] Integration into NATO will also include finishing the process of bringing key Baltic airfields and ports up to NATO standards to facilitate the rapid movement of personnel and equipment into the region.

In the scenario, the United States deploys ground forces that include two heavy divisions, an SBCT, an air assault division, an MEU, a PAC-3 Patriot brigade, a Special Forces group, and corps-level assets. Naval forces include an amphibious ready group, three or four Aegis cruisers or destroyers, and a squadron of P-3 maritime patrol aircraft. Air forces include 14 long-range bombers, more than four wings of tactical combat aircraft, a squadron of Predator UAVs with Hellfire missiles, and EA-6B jammers, E-3 AWACS, E-8

---

[2] Given Russia's procurement "bow-wave" and still limited procurement budget, it will be unable to expand its front-line submarine and aviation forces. By 2012 a handful of modern SSNs and conventional submarines (SSKs) will have replaced some of the older ships currently in service while Russian tactical aviation continues to rely on upgraded variants of the MiG-29, Su-27, and Su-30. During this period Russia will be unable to develop, procure, and field a fifth-generation fighter in operationally relevant numbers.

[3] As Poland and the Baltic states are well along in the process of integration into NATO, this would reflect a broadening and deepening of these efforts.

JSTARS, RC-135s, Global Hawk, tankers, and other supporting aircraft.

NATO Objectives, CONOPs, and Capabilities. NATO's objectives largely overlap with those of the United States. NATO aims to maintain the territorial and political integrity of the Baltic states, to ensure that they remain members of NATO, and to prevent either the horizontal or vertical escalation of the conflict. The overarching principle guiding the NATO CONOP is to deny the Russians access to as much of the territory of the Baltic states as possible while delaying the Russian advance and degrading Russian combat power with NATO air strikes and long-range fires. Offensive ground combat is to be engaged in only as a last resort because NATO plans to force the Russians into making a choice between conducting costly ground assaults with their degraded force or initiating peace negotiations on terms favorable to NATO. Should either of these two events fail to occur, NATO will go on the offensive to liberate any Baltic state territory still occupied by the Russian Army.

Britain contributes an armored division, four guided-missile destroyers, and a wing of Tornado strike aircraft. Germany contributes a Panzer division; some guided-missile frigates, minesweepers, and diesel attack submarines; and a wing of Tornado strike/suppression of enemy air defenses aircraft. The Dutch also contribute frigates and, with the Norwegians, a squadron of F-16s. Canada contributes CF-18s. Poland contributes a mechanized infantry brigade, and the Finns and Swedes contribute elements of their Nordic Brigade outside of NATO command.

Baltic Objectives, CONOPs, and Capabilities. The primary conflict objectives of the Baltic states are to preserve their political independence and territorial integrity while minimizing the casualties suffered by their populations. They will also seek to maximize NATO involvement in their defense to ensure that no political deals are cut at their expense and to seek maximum destruction of Russian military power to prevent a repeat of the Russian invasion at some future date. The Baltic brigade and other assets are presumed to play a role in resisting Russian aggression.

Findings

In sum, our analysis of Russian threats and U.S. and coalition vulner-abilities concluded that the Russian military's anti-access capabilities are limited by a continuing state of decline that is now more than a decade old. While pockets of technical excellence exist in both it and the Russian defense industry, the chronic and difficult-to-reverse weaknesses of the Russian military limit the potential operational effectiveness of a Russian military anti-access strategy and leave IO and PSYOPS as Russia's most effective potential anti-access strategy.

Key Access Issues

In-Theater Access Issues. Our analysis suggests that, for the United States and its allies, the greatest anti-access in-theater vulnerability is concentrated in the area of the Baltic Sea. If Russia could find a suc-cessful combination of mines, submarines, and air-launched antiship missiles, it could potentially deny NATO forces access to the eastern Baltic Sea for a protracted period. This ability probably would render moot the seizure of a coastal foothold in the Baltic states by the USMC because by the time NATO forces cleared the area of subma-rines and mines and reduced the threat of air-launched antiship mis-siles to a manageable level, the land campaign would be well under way and most of the region already liberated. In addition, these same capabilities could prevent U.S. lift operations into Poland's eastern Baltic Sea ports once hostilities have begun.[4]

En-Route Access Issues. The en-route base infrastructure avail-able for this deployment is robust and both of limited significance and generally immune to attack. Airlifted U.S. personnel and equip-ment can deploy, if necessary, directly from CONUS to Western Europe but with a noticeable loss of C-17A and C-5 lift capacity.[5] However, alternative en-route bases are available to mitigate these

---

[4] These ports, particularly Gdansk and Gdynia, would also be vulnerable to attacks from Kaliningrad.

[5] The reason is that the longer ranges associated with direct flights require a trade-off with the average weight that can be carried.

impacts. The air deployment to Poland will require en-route bases but, as with Western Europe, multiple alternatives exist, should operations at either Lajes Field, the Azores, or RAF Mildenhall be disrupted.

Furthermore, it would be very difficult for the few Russian submarines potentially operating in the area to locate, track, and target U.S. lift ships as they cross the Atlantic Ocean. Given the small number of operational Russian submarines (fewer than 20 operational SSNs in the Northern and Pacific Fleets), their relatively low survival rates, and the difficulty they will have in locating their targets, Russia would be unlikely to intercept a single lift ship let alone effectively interdict the sea lines of communication (SLOCs) to Europe.[6] Similar logic holds for Russia's long-range maritime strike aircraft, except they are less stealthy than Russian submarines. The Russian Navy's 45 Tu-22M "Backfire" bombers lack the range to strike at the SLOCs to Europe from their home airfields, and will need to be redeployed to western Russia to be able to interdict the maritime approaches to Europe.[7] Russia's lack of an effective maritime surveillance capability will mean that there is only a small probability of any Tu-22M sortie locating U.S. sealift ships among the

---

[6] The Russian submarine fleet has shrunk significantly from its Cold War peak. About 20 SSNs and 16 SSKs are currently operational in the Russian Navy. We assume that Russia's submarine force will stabilize at about 15 SSNs and 11 SSKs in a fleet consisting of the *Oscar II*, *Akula*, and *Kilo* classes (*Jane's Fighting Ships 2002–2003*). Submarines currently in reserve or waiting refit will be scrapped in order to focus on introducing the *Yasen* and *Lada* classes. These newer classes will replace the current fleet on a one-for-one basis throughout the period being considered. Our estimate as to the survivability of Russian submarines is based on the opinion of an experienced serving naval submariner who was a member of our analysis team. His estimate was based on the important caveat that the USN continue to practice and maintain its ASW (subsurface, surface, and air) skills.

[7] We assume that the Russian Air Force's "Backfire" regiments lack the training necessary to conduct maritime strike operations and that they will be involved in strike operation more directly supporting Russian ground operations. The combat radius of the Tu-22M-3 is 810 to 900 nautical miles in a lo-lo-lo profile (the profile this aircraft is likely to use to penetrate NATO's continental air defense barriers) and 1,300 nautical miles for a hi-hi-hi profile. Even with longer range, Tu-22Ms operating from western Russia can just reach the entrance to the English Channel. These ranges also make it impossible for the "Backfire" to avoid NATO air defenses by flying a circuitous route around Norway (*Jane's All the World's Aircraft 2000–2001*).

dense maritime traffic in the approaches to the English Channel and the North Sea. This will result in the need for multiple sorties through defended NATO airspace (both land- and carrier-based) and the rapid attrition of Russia's small maritime strike force.[8]

Poland's land transportation infrastructure is very important to this operation because it provided the only means of reaching NATO's assembly areas near the Lithuanian border. Thus, Poland's railways, roads, and bridges need to be strong enough to support the eastward movement of NATO's heavy equipment. Should this infrastructure prove inadequate, significant additional time will be needed to make the improvements necessary to support NATO's deployment operations. Furthermore, it is important that redundant suitable routes eastward are available to avoid creating a small number of chokepoints that can be destroyed by Russia or at which concentrations of NATO units will form that can be targeted by Russian area attack submunitions. This study was unable to determine the extent to which the Polish transportation system could support the eastward movement of V Corps and has assumed that it is sufficient for the operation.[9] If this is not the case, U.S. movements through Poland may be considerably slower than expected and more susceptible to Russian interdiction and sabotage.

CONUS Access Issues. Given Russia's lack of conventional strategic reach, operationally significant anti-access attacks within CONUS appear unlikely. Russia will rather try to disrupt the deployment with computer network attack operations aimed at computer networks of organizations supporting the deployment, and it may try to harass U.S. SPOEs and APOEs with SOF or irregular attacks. The direct effects of such operations are likely to be minor because U.S. forces frequently train for this sort of contingency. An

---

[8] Penetrating Russian aircraft would first need pass through NATO's frontline defenses, then through NATO SAM belts, and finally the rear area defenses provided by the United Kingdom, the Benelux states, and U.S. carrier air wings providing escort and defense for U.S. lift ships. This gauntlet would then have to be run in reverse as the Tu-22Ms return to their bases in Russia.

[9] It is our understanding, however, that NATO is making important infrastructure improvements to Poland's transportation infrastructure.

important exception to this would be a successful surprise attack on U.S. lift ships prior to their mobilization which renders a number of them inoperable. Because these vessels are in limited supply damaging a number of the larger ships could prolong the deployment process.[10]

Threats of Greatest Concern

We judged that the main Russian threats to U.S. access in the Baltics scenario were IO and PSYOPS, air-launched antiship cruise missiles, sea mines, and a rapid ground offensive.

IO and PSYOPS. The Russian anti-access strategy with the greatest potential effect would be a political strategy intended to separate the United States from its key access-related European NATO allies: Germany, Belgium, and the Netherlands. While Russia does possess military capabilities that could allow it to impede the movement of U.S. forces into the theater of operations, such a strategy would be unlikely to have a militarily useful result or alter the ultimate outcome of a future NATO-Russia conflict. Only by using IO and PSYOPS to create the conditions (or take advantage of existing conditions) for exploiting a strategic rift between the United States and its NATO allies can Russia hope to successfully implement a strategically meaningful anti-access strategy.

The potential threat in Germany was believed to be especially important because a successful Russian campaign might help mobilize anti-war activists there, either to put pressure on their government to withdraw its support for the U.S.-led operation or to conduct a campaign of civil disobedience that would delay the deployment of V Corps. Militarily, the gravest threat to U.S. deployment operations would be for the German government to prevent the deployment of V Corps from its German cantonments to eastern Poland. Replacing these units with CONUS-based ones would not only require a great deal of additional lift (about 35 notional roll-on/roll-off vessels [RO/ROs]), it also would strain the U.S. Army, which has only three CONUS-based heavy divisions—a strain that would be even greater

---

[10] It is assumed that once these ships have been moved to port and begun loading operations they will be harder to target because of dispersal and better protection.

if a U.S. heavy division were required to replace the German Panzer division in the NATO order of battle. The loss of Germany's rail network would be a manageable nuisance because longer and less dense rail networks that circumvent Germany do exist. However, although neither of these occurrences is a show-stopper, they both have the potential to seriously delay the deployment of U.S. forces to eastern Poland and to increase the time and cost required to liberate the Baltic states.

The individual loss of either Belgium or the Netherlands would not have as great an impact and might be considered little more than an inconvenience, leading to the need to find additional berths in the region and perhaps resulting in a slight delay in the deployment time lines. However, the loss of both states would potentially disrupt the deployment time lines because less-suitable ports, most likely further west in France, would need to be used.

The Russian IO and PSYOPS campaign would not need to convince governments to withdraw their support for the NATO operations to be a successful anti-access strategy. It could also succeed if it mobilized antiwar or anti-American groups to protest against NATO operations in the Baltic region. Such protests could affect the U.S. deployment in two different ways. First, they could lead to direct acts of civil disobedience, such as blocking railways and base access or even sabotage, that interfere with the U.S. deployment. The effectiveness of such tactics would depend both on the scale of the protest actions and on the willingness and ability of the local or national governments to contain them. Depending on the context of the protests, host-nation civil and military authorities might be reluctant to confront them in a timely or effective fashion. Second, mass political protests might lead governments to hesitate in making decisions necessary for the efficient deployment or transit of U.S. forces. Even if brief, such hesitations would increase the length of time necessary for force closure in eastern Poland.

It was the opinion of the anti-access team that while the potential for a successful Russian IO and PSYOPS operation existed, this possibility was highly context-dependent.[11] Ultimately the team concluded that this was the greatest Russian anti-access threat, particularly in 2012 and beyond, not because of its likelihood but because of its significant effects should it come to pass.

The most serious, and least likely, political anti-access threat was the possibility that Poland would deny NATO access to its territory. This denial would most likely be a show-stopper, for it would leave NATO without a land border contiguous with the Baltic States. While NATO could attempt to insert forces by amphibious or airborne assault, the success of such operations would be highly problematic (at least in the short- and medium-term future) given Russia's abilities to deny NATO access to the eastern Baltic Sea and to create a sophisticated IADS in the region using its mobile advanced SAMs. It is difficult to foresee, however, circumstances under which Poland would be unwilling to give its full support to an American-sponsored operation or in which a Russian IO and PSYOPS campaign would find much traction with the Polish population or among Polish political elites in the time frame examined here.[12]

Air-Launched Antiship Cruise Missiles. Air-launched antiship cruise missiles were judged to be a problem within the confines of the Baltic Sea because Russia is developing some very advanced models that can maneuver in flight and have very long ranges (more than 150

---

[11] Germany has a strong Green Party and well-organized and popularly supported peace movements that could be exploited by Russian IO and PSYOPS. Were Russian IO and PSYOPS to generate within Germany significant hostility towards the U.S.-led operation, a campaign of civil unrest with the ability to impede the deployment of U.S. military from and through Germany could ensue. The delays resulting from such a campaign can potentially be prolonged by the likely reluctance of the German government to risk physical harm to the protesters and the possibility that its willingness to take strong measures might be lackluster. This threat was considered to be even greater in the 2012 period because of the possibility that a long-term chronic decline in the perception among the European populace and important European political actors about the commonality of interests with the United States could leave Europe—in particular Germany—more vulnerable to Russian IO and PSYOPS. By this time, the perceptual rift between the United States and Germany might be wide enough that the German government would prevent the deployment of V Corps from its bases in Germany and that it would not allow U.S. forces to transit its territory to attack.

[12] This assumption is based on our understanding of Poland's historical experience with Russia and its strong support of the United States.

miles). They could be launched by heavy bombers or larger tactical aircraft, such as the Su-30, from outside the main defensive envelope of a U.S. amphibious ready group and used to control SLOCs. If many were fired in a saturation attack, U.S. defenses could be overwhelmed and a few missiles could strike their targets, causing significant casualties.

Even should the United States decide not to put amphibious ships in the Baltic, antiship cruise missiles would threaten NATO minesweepers and ASW ships on patrol. These weapons bear watching because Russia could begin to field long-range maritime strike aircraft in operationally effective numbers and develop a survivable maritime area surveillance capability and could become a blue water (open ocean), rather than green water (littoral seas), threat. It is unlikely, however, that Russia can field such systems in the foreseeable future in sufficient numbers to be able to saturate the air defense systems of a carrier battle group or the potential Aegis escorts protecting sealift ships in the Atlantic Ocean.

Sea Mines. Russia also could attempt to covertly deploy advanced sea mines in a crisis, either from diesel submarines or military-owned merchant ships disguised as civilian vessels. These mines could block access to large Polish SPODs (such as Gdynia), for which some American heavy equipment sets would be destined at the outset of hostilities. Mines could also block the entrance to some of the main Baltic ports, such as Liepaja and Tallinn, thus making a prospective amphibious assault even more difficult.

Russian Ground Offensive. Finally, any rapid Russian ground offensive would be a potent anti-access tool as well. This stems from the geography of the theater. To push into the heartland of the Baltics, NATO ground forces would have to move through a narrow corridor of southern Lithuania that lies between the Kaliningrad enclave and Belarus.[13] If Russian ground forces were to pinch off this narrow corridor with a quick ground offensive (or with effective long-range fires), NATO ground forces would be denied access to the Bal-

---

[13] The land corridor between Russia and Kaliningrad encompasses all of Lithuania and part of Latvia.

tic states until they successfully fought their way through the Russian blocking forces. This could be a prolonged and bloody affair that would give other Russian forces the opportunity to occupy most of the Baltic states.

Other Threats Considered

Attack Submarines. Although Russia possesses a variety of relatively modern SSN and nuclear-powered, guided-missile (SSGN) classes armed with advanced torpedoes and antiship missiles, these vessels were considered only a secondary threat to inbound U.S. strategic lift ships for a variety of reasons. These reasons included the limited number of such vessels available to Russia (because few are left in service, they are geographically dispersed, and even fewer are operational because of training and funding problems), the difficulty in locating and targeting U.S. lift ships in the crowded English Channel and North Sea SLOCs, the difficulty that Russian submarines will have in penetrating NATO layered ASW defenses, and the difficulty they will have in surviving once they begin to attack U.S. shipping. All of these factors combined make it unlikely that the United States will lose a lift ship to a Russian submarine.

However, because the loss of a single lift ship carrying hard-to-replace equipment (e.g., M1A2 tanks, Patriot missile batteries) could delay the closure of the deployment and the start of the operation, Russian submarines operating in the vicinity of the North Sea SPODs were considered to be a secondary threat. They were considered a secondary threat because, although the threat they present to U.S. deployment operations cannot be ignored, they are both manageable with existing capabilities and unlikely to be a show-stopper. The extent of this threat is also largely mitigated by the fact that Russian submarines would not begin operating against U.S. lift ships until at least 30 days after the start of the U.S. deployment. Therefore, the bulk of the deployment will have already been finished before Russian attacks commence, and NATO will have had a great deal of time to scour the approaches to the North Sea SPODs and to ensure that they were clear of lurking Russian submarines. The Russian submarine fleet was downgraded to the tertiary level in 2012 because it was expected that Russian submarine numbers would continue to decline because of funding difficulties and the failure to build new ships in adequate numbers. This decline is also caused by expected improvements in U.S. ASW capabilities, primarily through the introduction of the new *Virginia*-class submarines.

SOF. The improvement in Russian SOF and irregular forces is predicated on the reconstruction of the Cold War networks of saboteurs and arms caches in Western Europe springing from an assumed decline in Russian-NATO relations in the period after 2007.[14] This improvement in capability could better Russia's ability to interfere with U.S. deployment operations in Western Europe. However, the effects of such operations will remain modest because of the redundancy of the region's transportation infrastructure and Russia's reluctance to engage in open hostilities prior to the completion of its military mobilization. The most important threats identified were SRBM and SOF and irregular attacks on the region's transportation infrastructure, submarine attacks on ships operating in the eastern Baltic Sea, and Russia's advanced air-to-surface antiship capabilities.

Land-Attack Cruise Missiles. The introduction of long-range and highly accurate conventional air-launched cruise missiles fitted with submunitions could give Russia the ability to deny NATO the use of Poland's airfields and ports. This threat was assessed as being secondary because NATO will have finished using the Polish APODs and SPODs for deployment before hostilities commence, usable Polish airfields are numerous, the damage is readily repairable, and strategic deployment directly into Poland is not necessary for the rapid closure of NATO forces at their tactical assembly area around Suwalki. Moreover, the greatest possibility for Russian anti-access success in the Polish theater will be its ability to temporarily close the Polish ports of Gdynia and Gdansk.

---

[14] See, for example, Christopher Andrew and Vasili Mitrokhin, *The Sword and Shield: The Mitrokhin Archive and the Secret History of the KGB*, New York: Basic Books, 1999; Graham Turbinville, "3 Prototypes for Targeting America: A Soviet Assessment," *Military Review*, January–February 2002, available at http://www.cgsc.army.mil.

These weapons have the range, the large warheads, and the accuracy (25-meter CEP for the Kh-55SE and 6- to 20-meter CEP, depending on the source, for the Kh-101) to make them effective against lift ships moored in the primary European SPODs. Coupled with the Tu-22M5 "Backfire" and a modernized ISR network, these weapons could make an effective killer of moored LMSRs.[15] They could also be used to scatter submunitions that could damage or destroy important MHE and degrade general port operations. Should this be the case, either developing a deployable anti–cruise missile capability or providing lift ships with active and passive defenses, may become an urgent priority, particularly because these missiles are likely to be made available to other states. By 2012, the study team judged the Russian threat to increase because of the introduction of LACMs or conventional air-launched cruise missiles.

Long-Range SAMs. Russia's ability to build an IADS in the region would complement its anti-access strategies by interfering with NATO's anti-anti-access operations. The long range of these systems, particularly those expected to be introduced in the future, would force NATO ISR and C2/battlefield management aircraft to stay back from the area of operations, thus complicating the search for Russian mobile SRBMs and SAMs and the detection of penetrating Russian aircraft.[16] These systems could also threaten NATO airborne ASW and MCM operations off the coast of the Baltic states and, in the future, operations from airfields in eastern Poland. As a result, a lengthy—and by no means certain—suppression of enemy air defenses (SEAD) campaign might be required before some U.S. anti-anti-access capabilities can be utilized effectively. By extending the length of the SEAD campaign, Russian long-range SAMs would facilitate other Russian anti-access capabilities by making it more difficult to detect and intercept penetrating Russian aircraft and to

---

[15] These missiles are reported to use TV picture comparison for terminal guidance, which would suggest a need for fairly up-to-date imagery. The Kh-55SE is also mentioned as possibly having an active radar terminal seeker for use against ships.

[16] These ranges, however, do not give Russian SAMs the ability to interfere directly with U.S. deployment operations.

locate and target mobile SRBM launchers and by delaying the start of ASW and MCM operations in the littoral waters of the Baltic states. Thus, while Russian long-range SAMs are not in and of themselves an anti-access threat, they can increase the survivability, and thus the potential effectiveness, of existing Russian anti-access systems.

Implications for Regional Commanders

This scenario reinforced the team's perceptions about the significant advantages to be derived from forward deployment. These advantages include having useful military capabilities already in theater that can be deployed tactically and that do not require strategic deployment assets, the need to move fewer heavy forces by strategic lift, a more rapid closure time, and less probability of a catastrophic loss of equipment from the destruction of a single RO/RO or other high-value strategic mobility target. As one would expect, forward deployment also limits an opponent's ability to adopt a successful anti-access strategy by providing useful in-theater capabilities to counter such an effort.

Access Requirements

In our Baltics scenario, the commander of EUCOM would face two primary access requirements: securing the major highways and railroad lines across Germany and Poland and securing and protecting major Polish APODs. In addition, there is a secondary requirement to maintain control of the key Baltic sea lanes.

Securing Major Highways and Railroad Lines Across Germany and Poland. The need to secure the major highways and railway lines across Germany and Poland derives from the requirement to move elements of two American heavy divisions from base areas in western Germany to the Polish-Lithuanian border as well as the need to move the equipment sets of the heavy U.S. brigades and corps combat support and combat service support assets arriving by sea from CONUS from German and Dutch ports to eastern Poland. Virtually all the American vehicles and most ammunition and fuel would move to Poland on European rolling stock or by road, if necessary.

Protecting Major Polish APODs. It is important to secure and protect major Polish APODs because they would host the bulk of American and NATO tactical air power in the theater during a Baltics contingency. Any degradation of the capacity of the major Polish air bases for hosting advanced tactical aircraft would force NATO air power to stand off at distances that might reduce sortie rates and increase tanker requirements. Any damage to these Polish APODs would slow the flow of personnel and equipment into Poland.

Maintaining control of the Baltic sea lanes is only a secondary requirement because such control would only be necessary if the commander of EUCOM wished to mount an amphibious assault on the Lithuanian coast at the outset of the campaign. Because such an assault is deemed unlikely by the project team, we saw no justification for making this a primary requirement. Such an assault would not be essential for NATO mission success and, even were the sea lanes to be largely cleared, a risk would remain that one or two Russian diesel submarines or a handful of air-launched antiship cruise missiles would get through the NATO naval screen and inflict damage on one or more ships in the USMC amphibious ready group.

Requirements of Allies. In our Baltics scenario, the commander of EUCOM would require that the European NATO allies, primarily Germany, the Netherlands, Belgium, and Poland, give U.S. forces full access to their ports, air bases, highways, and railroads.

Polish air bases would be essential to NATO and U.S. tactical air operations over the Baltics. APODs, SPODs, highways, and railroads in the Netherlands, Belgium, and Germany would be indispensable to the reception of ground forces arriving from CONUS and to the onward movement of both CONUS-based and Germany-based ground forces. This requirement for full access in Europe is the most important one that the EUCOM commander would place on our major NATO allies.

Another way in which the NATO allies could help EUCOM to be successful in our Baltics scenario would be by contributing capable heavy ground and tactical air units to the actual operations in the theater. The U.K., Germany, and France have the most capable militaries in NATO outside the United States, so they would have the greatest potential contributions to make. If each of these countries could contribute two or three brigades' worth of heavy ground forces and one wing equivalent of ground-attack aircraft, the task facing the commander of EUCOM would become much easier, because less U.S. equipment would need to be moved from CONUS. As revealed by the scenario, opportunities exist for allies to contribute important niche capabilities as well. For example, MCM, ASW, SOF, offensive counterair, SEAD, SAM capabilities, AWACS, and the potential for a future NATO capability akin to JSTARS all could represent important European contributions in a Baltics campaign.

Options for the Commander of EUCOM

IO and PSYOPS. Perhaps the most important counter that the EUCOM commander could use would be an effective IO and PSYOPS program designed to maintain European (especially German) political support for the mission to defend the Baltics. Such a program would have to be directed at both European governments and publics and conducted in an integrated fashion with broader U.S. public diplomatic efforts. Government support alone might not be enough to guarantee complete and easy access to transportation infrastructures. If European publics (especially in Germany) remain largely hostile to the Baltics mission, large civil disobedience and passive resistance campaigns could be mounted that would disrupt the movement of U.S. forces across the continent by road and rail.

Capable Heavy Ground Forces. As mentioned earlier, one of the principal threats to U.S. and NATO access to the Baltics is a rapid Russian ground offensive to cut off the narrow corridor of southern Lithuania near the Polish border.

Clearly, the most effective counter to this threat would be well-trained and synchronized NATO heavy armored forces that break through any Russian blocking effort quickly by coordinating deep fires with close combat operations. The key to success here would be high levels of force compatibility and interoperability among American, British, German, and French heavy forces.

Attack Submarines (SSNs). Another important counter would be the deployment of a handful of nuclear attack submarines (U.S. and British) into the Baltic Sea to prevent Russian diesel submarines from operating there. By clearing the Baltic Sea of Russian diesels, NATO would minimize the threat to its minesweepers working to clear key SPODs of Russian mines. This measure might allow the Commander of EUCOM to move some U.S. amphibious ships into the Baltic Sea to threaten an amphibious assault on the Baltic coast.[17]

---

[17] Even if an amphibious assault is not intended, the mere presence of an afloat Marine Expeditionary Brigade in the region could divert Russian attention from NATO ground attacks, much as in the situation in Operation Desert Storm, where the presence of an afloat U.S. Marine brigade in the Persian Gulf drew the Iraqis' attention away from the western desert where the famous "Left Hook" offensive was being prepared.

CHAPTER SIX

Latin America and the Caribbean

This chapter details our gaming of a number of lower-intensity scenarios in the SOUTHCOM area of responsibility. We first provide an overview of the games, including descriptions of potential U.S. adversaries' capabilities; summarize our findings; and detail the implications for access requirements and options available to reduce the efficacy of regional anti-access strategies.

Overview of the Games

The Latin America (Central and South America) and the Caribbean anti-access game presented an opportunity for a brief consideration of a range of potential scenarios relating to the region. In developing these scenarios, we recognized that U.S. forces would face a much more permissive anti-access environment than is found in Southwest Asia, East Asia, or the former Soviet Union. The overall military technological level in the region is low, and many of the conventional militaries of the area are organized and trained primarily for internal security operations. However, the region does host a smattering of malevolent guerrilla and terrorist groups who might choose to employ unorthodox tactics (such as mass hostage seizures) to render access unpleasant for U.S. military forces during any contingency in the next decade.

The Scenarios

Our approach to the Latin America work was different than that taken in the other regions we studied in this report. Instead of focusing on one dominant scenario, we chose to lightly examine a range of possible scenarios with an eye toward picking out any long poles in the tent that U.S. commanders might need to think about when planning any future operations in Latin America that require significantly expanded access.

Our reasoning was that no dominant threat source or scenario exists in Latin America as it does in East Asia or Southwest Asia. Instead, planners need to consider a host of potential "messy little contingencies" when thinking about access requirements and threats in the region.

We examined three scenarios at the high end of the spectrum:

- an intervention in a Cuban Civil War;
- an invasion of Venezuela; and
- a full blown counterinsurgency campaign against the Revolutionary Armed Forces of Colombia (FARC) rebels in Colombia.

We also examined four additional scenarios at the low end of the spectrum:

- a counterterrorist campaign against Middle Eastern terrorist groups in the tri-border region of Argentina, Brazil, and Paraguay;
- expanded counterdrug operations across the Andes region;
- a noncombatant evacuation operation (NEO) in Venezuela; and
- an NEO in Colombia in the event of a FARC campaign to conduct mass seizures of U.S. hostages.

Potential Adversaries in Latin America and the Caribbean

Adversaries that the United States might face in the region consist of weak conventional militaries with largely underdeveloped navies and air forces, guerrilla/terrorist groups, drug cartels and organized crime, and right-wing militias. Because of the range of potential adversaries and number of scenarios covered, we present a brief description of the key actors in the region rather than following the more detailed formula ("Actors, Objectives, CONOPs, and Capabilities") used in previous chapters.

Indigenous Guerrilla and Terrorist Groups

The most threatening guerrilla organization in Latin America is clearly the leftist FARC, who have been conducting a long-running insurgency against the Colombian government. Also of concern, but much less threatening at the moment, are the Colombian Ejercito Liberación National (ELN) and the Maoist Shining Path movement in Peru.

FARC. The FARC is a capable, well-organized guerrilla force of about 15,000, which has historically pursued its objective of overturning the Colombian government by carrying out overwhelming attacks against isolated police stations, army outposts, and government buildings in remote rural provinces.[1] Until the mid-1990s, the FARC operated in relatively small units with only rudimentary weapons, but, in recent years, fueled by an influx of revenue from "taxes" levied on coca growers, the FARC has deployed more advanced and innovative weapons and begun to attack with larger (battalion-size) units. In addition, the group has started to accelerate the pace of its urban guerrilla operations.[2]

Although the FARC still relies mainly on small arms to fight government forces, it has other assets that might be of value in anti-access type attacks. These include man-portable air defense systems, improvised explosive devices (IEDs) with innovative trigger mecha-

---

[1] For operational details on the FARC, see Angel Rabasa and Peter Chalk, *Colombian Labyrinth: The Synergy of Drugs and Insurgency and Its Implications for Regional Stability*, Santa Monica, Calif.: RAND Corporation, MR-1339-AF, 2001, Chapters Three and Four.

[2] For a discussion of the FARC's move into urban areas, see Jeremy McDermott, "FARC Gives Notice of an Urban Campaign," *Jane's Intelligence Review*, September 2002, pp. 24–25.

nisms, medium-range rockets, and mortars.[3] In addition to this increasingly potent weaponry, the FARC has also been known to use kidnapping and hostage-taking tactics to put pressure on its enemies.

ELN and Shining Path. Neither Colombia's ELN nor Peru's Shining Path is as well equipped or as tactically sophisticated as the FARC. Both organizations are also much smaller than the FARC in terms of both size and area of active operations. These groups have sought to sabotage industrial infrastructure, intimidate local civilians, and assault small military outposts, using small footborne units of irregulars. Their military capabilities are thus quite limited.

Nonindigenous Guerrilla and Terrorist Groups

In addition to the indigenous terrorist organizations just discussed, a number of nonindigenous guerrilla and terrorist groups have been reported by credible sources to be operating in the area. Apparently, the most well-entrenched group in Latin America is the Lebanese Hezbollah. However, the Egyptian Islamic Group also reportedly has an infrastructure in the region.

The Middle Eastern terror groups in Latin America have traditionally been concentrated in the tri-border area where Argentina, Brazil, and Paraguay meet. The power of national governments is weak in this region, leading to the proliferation of such illegal activities as smuggling and narcotrafficking. Hezbollah in particular has also taken advantage of a significant Arab expatriate population in the tri-border area to build its support and operational infrastructure. However, none of the nonindigenous groups operating in the region possesses significant military capabilities of the sort necessary to sustain a significant military campaign.

In recent months, open-source media accounts indicate that, as a result of increasing pressure from local law enforcement, Middle Eastern terror groups in Latin America have dispersed their networks to new areas of operation, specifically the Brazilian Amazon, northern Chile, and the Brazilian financial center of Sao Paolo.

---

[3] Toxic weaponry also are available. A discussion of the global trend toward toxic warfare is found in Karasik (2002).

Regional Conventional Militaries

Of all the states in Latin America, only Cuba and Venezuela were identified by the project team as potential military adversaries of the United States.[4] However, both militaries have relatively weak naval and air capabilities, so neither would present a serious conventional threat to U.S. forces. It appears that Venezuela's capabilities are somewhat greater than those of Cuba.

Cuba. Eleven years after the collapse of their Soviet patron, the Cuban Navy and Air Force are both in a fairly decrepit state.

The Cuban Navy possesses only four Osa II missile craft and one Pauk II coastal patrol craft. It also has some coastal artillery and antiship missile systems, none of which is technologically advanced.[5] The Cuban Air Force probably has only 25 operational fighter aircraft with which to challenge any U.S. intervention on the island.[6] These are largely old MiG-21 and -23 models that pose little danger to the more advanced U.S. fighter aircraft that would support any hypothetical American intervention.

One wild card that needs to be considered here is the extent of Cuba's WMD program. Little has been revealed in open sources about the extent of any chemical or biological weapons program Havana might have. If the Cubans do indeed possess significant stocks of either type of weapon, this would naturally complicate the question of Cuba's capabilities.

Venezuela. On paper, Venezuela's military capabilities appear to surpass those of Cuba. The Venezuelan Navy has two German-

---

[4] Under Fidel Castro, Cuba has continued to maintain a basically hostile posture toward the United States and has reached out to a number of virulently anti-American states and actors around the world, such as the FARC in Colombia, Iran, and Saddam Hussein's Iraq. Under President Hugo Chavez's rule, Venezuela has become an increasingly authoritarian state and more receptive to contacts with anti-American states around the world. Chavez maintains fairly close relations with Cuba and has met President Saddam Hussein of Iraq. Venezuela's current regime has also reportedly given shelter and sanctuary to FARC guerrilla units from Colombia.

[5] International Institute for Strategic Studies (IISS), *The Military Balance 2001–2002*, London, England: Oxford University Press, 2001, p. 230.

[6] IISS, p. 230.

manufactured diesel attack submarines that could threaten U.S. military sealift ships in the southern Caribbean. It also includes six *Mariscal Sucre* guided-missile frigates with surface-to-surface missiles, three missile attack craft, and three offshore patrol craft. The Venezuelan Air Force, meanwhile, has about 125 combat aircraft, including 16 CF-5s, 16 Mirage 50EVs, and 44 F-16A/Bs.[7] Some of these planes are equipped to fire Sidewinder air-to-air missiles and/or Exocet antiship missiles.

Findings

To summarize, project team members saw very little chance that any potential adversaries in the Latin American region could pose a significant military anti-access threat to the United States. None of the adversaries was believed capable of seriously disrupting the strategic movement of U.S. forces into the theater by sea and air. Only Venezuela has any appreciable naval and air assets with anti-access utility. However, most of these assets are a generation behind the U.S. platforms and systems that would be countering them. Also, it is not known whether the anti-access systems in the Venezuelan arsenal have been properly maintained over the years or if their crews have received adequate training in advanced combat tactics.

With the possible exception of Stingers and comparable man-portable air defense systems, the anti-access threats posed by indigenous and nonindigenous terrorist groups also were assessed to be minimal. None of the terrorist groups in Latin America has the capability to conduct a sustained anti-access campaign against U.S. forces. These organizations do, however, possess the potential to disrupt U.S. operations in the region, by conducting either a "terrorist spectacular" attack against U.S. forces at an APOD or SPOD (perhaps with a suicide bombing) or a low-level string of small pinprick attacks (e.g.,

---

[7] IISS, pp. 244–245.

snipings against individual GIs, small-unit attacks on isolated U.S. radar stations and surveillance outposts).

If military threats are generally low, U.S. interventions in the region would seem to be highly vulnerable to efforts that might exploit political vulnerabilities. Given the widespread perception of limited U.S. stakes or threats to the United States in the region and fears that U.S. forces were being sucked into a "quagmire," U.S. "will" to stay the course in jungle and mountain warfare could well be taxed.

Threats of Greatest Concern

The main anti-access threats in Latin America are primarily asymmetric in nature. These are harassment attacks against major APODs and SPODs, ambushes of American forces moving along transit routes, and mass hostage seizures of American civilians residing in the given country.

Harassment Attacks Against Major APODs/SPODs. Any of the posited Red forces in Latin America are unlikely to prevent U.S. forces from seizing the major APODs and SPODs that would be required for a given operation. However, both the conventional armies and guerrilla/terrorist groups in the region have the wherewithal to harass major ports and airfields with mortar fire, mines, IEDs, man-portable air defense systems, and sniper attacks. Local populations sympathetic to U.S. adversaries also might be mobilized to protest, riot, or overrun the APODs and SPODs or block lines of communication (LOCs), and labor stoppages by port or airfield workers could slow the throughput of materiel.

Attacks Along Transit Routes. Another potential weak point in the access equation for the United States involves the transit routes from major APODs and SPODs to the areas of active combat operations. In Latin America, a number of major airports are in the middle of large urban areas, so U.S. ground forces would have to move through densely populated urban terrain to get to the rural areas where many of the insurgents or guerrillas will have their principal bases and training camps. Hostile mobs or organized military opposition along these corridors could expose U.S. columns to ambushes with small arms, rocket-propelled grenades (RPGs), and IEDs, such as the ambushes in Mogadishu in 1993.

Other routes, including many of those from major SPODs to the interior of a country, pass through very dense jungled or mountainous terrain. These routes would provide numerous opportune ambush points for seasoned guerrilla and terrorist units as well as for more conventional units, such as those that might be fighting U.S. forces during any intervention in a post-Castro Cuban Civil War.

Hostage Seizures of American Civilians Residing in South America. A number of prominent Latin American guerrilla groups have a long history of using mass kidnappings as a way to attract attention to their cause and simultaneously demoralize their opponents. Both the FARC and ELN have used this tactic repeatedly. When this historical fact is coupled with the presence of large numbers of U.S. missionaries, relief workers, Drug Enforcement Administration agents, and oil company employees in remote rural areas throughout the region, there would seem to be a real opportunity for otherwise outgunned and outclassed guerrilla groups to even the playing field in a conflict by abducting U.S. civilians (possibly in the hundreds) as U.S. forces entered their country.

Implications for Regional Commanders

Access Requirements

The scenarios examined in this chapter lead to two overarching access requirements in the Latin American environment: securing main APODs and SPODs and securing transit routes.

Secure Main APODs and SPODs. Because of the potential for both conventional armies and guerrilla and terrorist groups to disrupt major ports and airfields, good perimeter security and solid cooperation with local authorities will be essential in any Latin American intervention. If key ports and airfields are not firmly secured early on, simple security requirements could consume increasingly large numbers of troops, thus decreasing the force available for actual combat operations.

Secure Transit Routes. The Latin American scenarios also require the commander of SOUTHCOM and the commander of ARSOUTH, to devote significant attention and resources to securing transit routes in areas of active combat operations. These routes could be scouted in advance using UAVs along with manned ISR platforms equipped with multispectral radar systems. Special Forces scout teams could also be inserted at key points along these routes to look for signs of enemy activity.

Once American units are established in an operational zone, the transit routes will likely turn into main supply routes and will require continuous monitoring to prevent any interruption of ground supply columns.

Requirements from Allies. The most important contribution the United States could receive from its allies in Latin America during counter anti-access operations would be up-to-date human intelligence reporting on the dispositions and intentions of enemy forces, especially guerrilla forces with amorphous command structures and unorthodox orders of battle. The countries best positioned to help the United States in this way would be those hosting U.S. counterinsurgency efforts after they themselves have been engaged in long counterinsurgency campaigns against the same guerrilla adversary. Human intelligence would probably be much more useful than most technical means of intelligence gathering in terms of helping U.S. forces preempt anti-access moves launched by hostile nonstate actors.

Options for the Commander of SOUTHCOM

Political. Virtually all the hypothetical intervention scenarios discussed here require an effective U.S. IO and PSYOPS campaign. Most of the adversaries posited in our Latin American cases are already unpopular with large segments of the local population, and an effective IO and PSYOPS campaign could increase popular anger against these actors, rendering it very difficult for them to operate freely. For example, the FARC appears to be unpopular in the areas of Colombia it has controlled because of the terror and intimidation tactics it has used against civilians. Thus, a sustained IO and PSYOPS campaign in Colombia before any U.S. intervention might turn the population decisively against the FARC.

Military-Technical. The judicious deployment of Special Forces detachments on special reconnaissance missions also appears to be an important counter to anti-access threats in Latin America. Special Forces could scout transit routes and assist indigenous security personnel in monitoring the entrances to major ports and airfields being used by U.S. forces. Most, but not all, of the Special Forces personnel needed in our Latin America scenarios should be Latin America specialists with Spanish language skills and a good understanding of regional cultural norms and mores.

Finally, capable air mobile forces were deemed a useful anti-access counter in all of the Latin American scenarios. The jungled, mountainous terrain of much of the region and the undeveloped road and rail network in many places make air mobility an ideal tool with which to move infantry rapidly around a given theater to keep adversary forces off balance and on the defensive. Helicopters could also bring supplies to forward units and provide continual, rapid-response fire support to both U.S. and friendly government forces that are not within range of land-based artillery or seaborne fires. Units capable of nighttime air mobile insertions would be especially valuable in this theater.

CHAPTER SEVEN

What the Games Revealed About Anti-Access Threats

We now turn to pulling the various threads of our analysis together to highlight the implications for the Army and joint community.

We begin with the observation that in none of the cases we examined could the adversary use military means to prevent U.S. access or to substantially delay or degrade the buildup of U.S. land or other forces by attacking anti-access targets. In all cases, U.S. Army forces could gain needed access to the region or could improvise workarounds.

For the 2003–2012 period we examined, most adversaries seemed likely to lack the critical military capabilities that have the combination of qualitative (e.g., range, payload, accuracy, sensor-to-shooter integration, training of personnel) and quantitative (i.e., inventory numbers) characteristics needed to provide a high probability of being *militarily* effective against key anti-access targets.[1]

On the other hand, in each of the regional scenario-based games we conducted, the adversary had ample opportunities in each phase of the scenario—in peacetime, crisis, and conflict—to use various combinations of diplomatic, economic, and military means to erode U.S. support and access in the region by focusing efforts on strategic targets. Adversaries used trade and economic incentives, subversion from within and without, bribes and bullying, coercive use of military power, and various maneuvers to try to put the United States and its

---

[1] A very large inventory of relatively inaccurate ballistic missiles, for example, can provide a relatively high probability of destroying a specific target.

regional partners and allies on opposite sides of key security and other issues.[2]

The relative military ineffectiveness of attacks on anti-access targets and the ample opportunities to erode U.S. access through actions that manifest themselves in the political domain led to a key finding of the study: *For the period we examined, adversaries have more incentives to use anti-access military capabilities against regional leadership and population targets than to attempt to destroy critical airports, seaports, and other anti-access targets. Moreover, nonmilitary anti-access means may in fact prove more effective than military ones.*

We have a number of important caveats that temper this conclusion, however.

First, recall that the time horizon for our games was out to 2012—less than a decade away and a relatively short amount of time for developing or otherwise acquiring and fielding new capabilities. *Technological trends are such that anti-access capabilities could dramatically improve past the 2012 horizon we examined.* Thus, our conclusion suggests that the United States has some time to redress aspects of the current military anti-access problem, while monitoring and developing counters for new adversary capabilities, assuming that the frequently glacial pace of development programs can be improved.

Second, we generally assumed that the United States would act reasonably quickly on available warning. It is, however, possible that without a quick response, the access situation for the United States could deteriorate. This could occur either as a result of key U.S. partners' and allies' defenses being overwhelmed by attacks and an "access window" being closed or as a result of political calculations that, in light of U.S. dithering, regional partners' and allies' interests would be best served by accommodating the putative U.S. adversary.

Third, we generally assumed that U.S. military forces could continue operations both during and after anti-access attacks because of the availability of an extensive range of relatively easy-to-acquire

---

[2] In the Iraq game, for example, Iraq used various means to try to link the crisis to the Israeli-Palestinian conflict and to portray the United States as a Western interloper in Arab and Persian Gulf affairs.

capabilities—from chemical and biological self-protection and decontamination gear to port handling and material handling capabilities and airfield and runway hardening and repair capabilities. If these capabilities were not available or were not available in sufficient density, however, the impact of anti-access attacks could be far more consequential than suggested by our analyses.

Fourth, we judged that the psychological impacts of attacks on anti-access targets, whether on U.S. military personnel or indigenous airport and seaport workers, also could be substantial, even though they are among the most difficult to gauge. A second major conclusion, therefore, is that *attacks on bases and other infrastructure are more likely to prove successful for their psychological value than the military significance of what they can reliably destroy*.[3] In our scenarios, we generally assumed that military personnel at APODs and SPODs would continue to perform their duties in the face of attacks, for example, at the same time recognizing that either organizational procedures or human nature could impose stiff performance penalties. We also viewed indigenous airport and seaport workers to be potentially unreliable in the face of attacks, which led to some concern that the Army and joint community will need to consider appropriate hedging actions to deal with this sort of eventuality.[4]

In a similar vein, although we recognized their potential importance, we had a difficult time judging the potential effectiveness of "strategic spectaculars." Such events might, like the Scud missile that struck the Dhahran barracks during the Gulf War or the downing of an aircraft filled with deploying troops, cause a large number of casualties and could complicate the domestic political base of support for the war. Our general view was that in cases where U.S. interests were viewed as important and clear, as in the case of an Iraq that appeared

---

[3] Recall the discussion in Chapter Three that concluded that a concerted strategy of ballistic missile attacks on Saudi and other GCC airports and seaports would result in only a modest—and ephemeral—reduction in the flow of forces into the Gulf in comparison to a political decision by any of the GCC states to deny access.

[4] For example, the early deployment of port handling and material handling units would help to hedge against the possibility that local workers might flee in the face of attacks or go on strike.

to be on the verge of acquiring nuclear weapons, or where such attacks took place on U.S. soil, such events would most likely backfire on the adversary and cause a surge in support. In other cases, where the interests were not viewed as important or clear, such attacks might stiffen the resolve of some and erode that of others, with a net reduction in the overall levels of support.[5] Alternatively, such spectaculars could destroy substantial military capability, such as a mobility asset carrying critical equipment or materiel (e.g., the downing of an airlifter or the sinking of an LMSR or munitions ship).[6] Finally, it was easy for us to imagine that spectacular attacks could temporarily place commanders and their forces in a "primal crouch" in which deployment operations might be suspended until safety and security could be ensured, with resulting delays in force buildups.

Our third major conclusion, as illustrated in the preceding chapters, was that adversaries lack strategic reach and therefore appear to have limited opportunities outside of their immediate theater of operation. As described above, however, development of longer-range ballistic and cruise missiles and strategic SOF capabilities to enable out-of-area—or even homeland—attacks, as well as more sophisticated IO capabilities, could extend the reach of potential adversaries.

Anti-Access Threats of Greatest Concern

We now offer our "short list" of the worldwide anti-access threats of greatest concern but need first to offer two important caveats.[7]

---

[5] For analyses of the role of casualties and other factors in public support for U.S. military operations, see Eric V. Larson, *Casualties and Consensus: The Historical Role of Casualties in Domestic Support for U.S. Military Operations*, Santa Monica, Calif.: RAND Corporation, MR-726-RC, 1996; Eric V. Larson, "Putting Theory to Work: Diagnosing U.S. Public Opinion on the U.S. Intervention in Bosnia," in Miroslav Nincic and Joseph Lepgold, eds., *Being Useful: Policy Relevance and International Relations Theory*, Ann Arbor, Mich.: University of Michigan Press, 2000, pp. 174–233.

[6] Such spectaculars could be conducted in theater, en route, or even in the United States.

[7] While we believe that there is substantial congruence between our study and others on the question of the anti-access threats of greatest concern, some other studies have accented other threats. Owen Coté (2000), whose study accents the Navy's role in the new security envi-

First, any list that focuses on categories of weapons risks missing the larger point that weapon systems increasingly need to be embedded in a larger system-of-systems that includes effective (i.e., accurate, timely, and useful) ISR and command, control, and communications (C3). Perhaps even more important, such systems need to be embedded in human organizations staffed by well-trained personnel with well-refined procedures that employ these technologies—whether advanced or otherwise—in operationally useful ways.[8]

Second, a host of context-specific factors influenced which threats in fact turned out to be of greatest concern in each of our scenarios—adversary and friendly capabilities, geography, overall maturity and robustness of regional infrastructure, and the potential utility of different methods of underwriting coercion and other strategic maneuvering—and these threats differed somewhat from scenario to scenario.

Ballistic and Cruise Missiles: A Threat to Bases, Leaders, and Populations

Ballistic and cruise missiles are at the top of our list of anti-access threats of concern, primarily for their strategic (i.e., terror) value, but

---

ronment, views TBMs, double-digit SAMs, and diesel submarines as the key anti-access threat the United States faces. Christopher Bowie (2002), whose study examines the anti-access threat to theater air bases that might be faced by the Air Force, emphasizes, as we do, political threats as well as deep-strike systems such as longer-range ballistic and cruise missiles, Special Forces, and WMD.

[8] In the first volume of his series on World War II, Winston Churchill notes that both the British and Germans had radar as early as 1939, but it was only the British that managed to integrate their radar systems in such a way that radar warning information could be effectively used by Royal Air Force air defense aircraft. He writes: "The Germans would not have been surprised to hear our radar pulses [in the spring of 1939], for they had developed a technically efficient radar system which was in some respects ahead of our own. What would have surprised them, however, was the extent to which we had turned our discoveries to practical effect, and woven all into our general air defence system. In this we led the world, and it was operational efficiency rather than novelty of equipment that was the British achievement." See Winston S. Churchill, *The Second World War, Volume 1, The Gathering Storm*, New York: Houghton Mifflin Company, 1948, p. 156. See also Arthur H. Barber III and Delwyn L. Gilmore, "Maritime Access: Do Defenders Hold All the Cards?" *Defense Horizons*, Washington, D.C.: Center for National Security Policy, National Defense University, October 2001.

also for their potential utility against airfields; they appear to have less, but still some, potential utility against seaports.[9] Particularly worrisome would be ballistic missiles with nuclear warheads.[10]

Used as terror weapons, nonnuclear-tipped ballistic missiles and cruise missiles can coerce friendly leaders, alienate their core constituencies, and cow their populations or drive a wedge between them and their leaders. As the capability to achieve greater ranges improves, the utility of these weapons will increase. In a more strictly military application, they can disrupt the smooth flow of forces into a region by placing at risk air bases and airlifters, seaports and sealifters, and the workers needed to ensure a speedy U.S. deployment, and push U.S. forces (e.g., air forces) to operate from greater operational distances. And as the range of threat systems increases, they may make increasingly possible terror or other attacks on en-route targets as well.[11]

Adversaries have several alternatives for increasing the military utility of ballistic and cruise missiles to underwrite their anti-access strategies. At the "low end" of possibilities, they might seek to increase their inventories of somewhat inaccurate ballistic and/or

---

[9] Airfields typically present many more soft targets (e.g., aircraft) than do ports.

[10] As in the PRC-Taiwan scenario, we assumed that nuclear weapons would not be used, largely because of the U.S. deterrent. If they were used, however, we would expect their principal targets to include ports and airfields needed for a buildup, and the impact of their use on these targets would almost certainly be to deny the U.S. access to these bases and push U.S. forces to use other, more distant bases. Additionally, while we generally thought it unlikely, it also could result in a strategic-level decision by U.S. policymakers that the situation had escalated in ways that the U.S. commitment might be called into question. In such a circumstance, it cannot be entirely ruled out that the United States might decide to halt further deployments or even withdraw.

[11] Concerned primarily about anti-access attacks on airfields, Bowie (2002, p. iii) argues, "Many potential adversaries are increasing their emphasis on the procurement of ballistic and cruise missiles. Government intelligence forecasts anticipate adversaries possessing larger numbers of longer-range ballistic and cruise missiles. The proliferation of satellite navigation systems, submunition warheads, and re-entry vehicle guidance systems has the potential to increase dramatically ballistic missile accuracy and lethality. Long-range, land-attack cruise missiles, which in some cases offer even higher accuracy than ballistic missiles, continue to proliferate. In addition, the new generations of ballistic and cruise missiles entering service can be fired from mobile launchers, which are more difficult to locate and attack than fixed launch sites."

cruise missiles. A midlevel option would be to improve the area effects capabilities of missiles by adding cluster munitions or other payloads.[12] Another midlevel option available to wealthier adversaries would be to increase the precision of their missiles (e.g., with GPS or other higher-resolution guidance systems) and to develop a "system of systems" that would provide the needed C3ISR capabilities (e.g., geostationary satellites for observation, UAVs). This would enable them to use their more accurate missiles more effectively. At the high end, they might develop nuclear payloads.

Operational solutions to the problem of ballistic missiles include attacks on threat capabilities at every phase of their deployment and employment—such as prelaunch attacks on missiles and transporter-erector-launchers (TELs) in garrisons; en route to and at their firing positions; and during boost, midcourse, and terminal phases.[13] The ease with which ballistic missiles can be improved and the difficulty of developing effective counters complicate this problem, however. Operational solutions for cruise missiles similarly include attacks on platforms (e.g., aircraft and ships) and missiles at each phase. A less attractive operational solution is for strategic movements to terminate outside missile threat rings, with forces either self-deploying from there or using theater assets to move to combat positions.[14]

In terms of technology thrusts, this threat demands highly deployable expeditionary air and missile defense capabilities that can protect cities, APODs, and SPODs. These capabilities need to be well-integrated into a deployable joint and coalition layered defense

---

[12] Area effects also might be achieved with nuclear, biological, and chemical payloads, which therefore cannot be ruled out. However, the use of such unconventional payloads could represent a substantial escalatory step.

[13] Layered defenses are an essential element to successful defense against theater missiles. See Eric V. Larson and Glenn A. Kent, *A New Methodology for Assessing Multilayer Missile Defense Options*, Santa Monica, Calif.: RAND Corporation, MR-390-AF, 1994.

[14] An interesting concept that presented itself in the Iraq scenario was for attack helicopters (e.g., Apache and Comanche) to self-deploy from an APOD or SPOD outside of ballistic missile threat rings.

that includes joint warning, control, and engagement capabilities[15] and can be made interoperable with the air and missile defense capabilities of regional partners and allies. The Army provides a wide range of suitable capabilities, from attack helicopters and SOF that can undertake strikes, raids, and direct action to providing important midcourse and terminal defense capabilities in the overall joint layered defense architecture.

Extended-Range Surface-to-Air Missiles: A Threat to Air Mobility

A prominent feature of all of our scenarios was the concern that extended-range SAM capabilities might increasingly be available to contest the establishment of air superiority and supremacy or threaten ingressing mobility aircraft—and thereby delay the arrival of forces by airlift, or force them to operate from more remote bases.[16] While advanced, extended-range SAMs appear to be one of the most serious emerging anti-access threats, it is one that will be largely limited to theaters where the choice of APODs is restricted by geography or political constraints to airfields that are fairly far forward.

AMC airlifters—perhaps especially including Civil Reserve Air Fleet aircraft—do not typically operate in contested airspace, potentially leading to the self-imposition of "no-fly zones" until airborne and surface-to-air threats have been destroyed or suppressed. Even when the skies have been cleared of airborne threats, extended-range SAMs may place at risk Army SBCTs or Objective Force Brigade Teams that deploy directly into the combat zone.

---

[15] For example, the Air Force's Airborne Laser (ABL) and the Navy's Upper-Tier and Aegis systems.

[16] Recent events suggest that substantial concern about the employment of man-portable air defense systems against airlifters is also increasingly warranted. In 2002, a discarded man-portable air defense system tube was found outside Prince Sultan AB, Saudi Arabia, an airfield used by U.S. forces, and a Russian helicopter was shot down by Chechen rebels in late August 2002, killing 118. Thirteen Russians were killed a year earlier in September 2001 when a shoulder-filed missile shot down their helicopter. See Cable News Network, "FBI Warns of Shoulder-Fired Missiles Threat," reported by Jamie McIntyre, May 30, 2002, and CNN, "Missile Downed Russian Helicopter," August 30, 2002.

A number of operational solutions are available for dealing with this threat. For example, one can develop more robust SEAD capabilities to ensure that the SAMs, their radars, and control systems are destroyed, and a wide range of means are currently available for accomplishing this.[17] Because such campaigns can take precious time, it may be desirable for airlifters to use self-protection measures to thwart SAM threats and low-altitude terrain masking in final approach and descent to come in under threat radars. An even less-preferred approach would be to operate high-value strategic mobility aircraft outside SAM threat rings and use theater airlifters (i.e., C-130s) for the final leg, while attempting to fly below the threat.

Among the available technological solutions might be enhancing capabilities to attack and destroy SAMs, their radars, and control systems; enhancing airlifters' low-altitude terrain-hugging and self-protection capabilities; and various jamming and other EW capabilities that can disrupt their terminal guidance and operation. An even better option would be to persuade Russia to stop selling advanced SAMs on the open market. However, Russia's continuing reliance on arms exports to meet its hard currency needs would suggest that such efforts are unlikely to succeed.

Antiship Missiles, Attack Submarines, and Sea Mining: Threats to Sealift

In addition to the threat they might pose to the operations of such tactical maritime units as carrier battle groups and Marine amphibious ready groups, each of the scenarios also presented adversaries with opportunities to attack an exceedingly high-value class of mobility asset: LMSRs or other sealift ships. Of greatest concern in this regard, because of their range, were air-launched antiship missiles and attack submarines. The obvious cost-effectiveness to adversaries of sea min-

---

[17] For example, Air Force F-16CJ fighter aircraft; Navy, Marine, or joint EA-6Bs; Navy Tomahawk cruise missiles; or even Army long-range fires (e.g., MLRS, ATACMS) might be used, and this might be a future area for the use of unmanned combat aerial vehicles (UCAVs). During the first Gulf War, Air Force MH-53J Pave Low helicopters and Army AH-64 Apache helicopters were employed against the Iraqi IADS. There is no reason that SOF could not also be used in a direct-action role against these targets.

ing also was readily apparent in the scenarios, although we generally viewed this as more of a nuisance and means of delaying deploying forces than as a serious threat.[18] The requirement for an attack capability against such targets includes, however, a robust and timely C3ISR—a capability that will only come at great expense and may therefore be an unattractive option for many potential future adversaries.

Counters for Antiship Missiles. As with ballistic, cruise, and extended-range surface-to-air missiles, the best operational means for overcoming antiship missiles will be to destroy them before they can be used. A second-best approach will be to provide escorts with self-defense capabilities (e.g., Aegis platforms) that can defend against air-to-surface missile attacks, or even enhancing the self-defense capabilities of LMSRs. The least-best operational solution will be to operate outside of air-to-surface missile threat rings.

Potential technological means for overcoming these threats include EW capabilities that can jam or disrupt missile guidance, avionics, or propulsion systems.

Counters for Attack Submarines. The Navy has robust ASW capabilities resident in its surface, undersea, and naval aviation communities, but continued capabilities in this area hinge on maintaining historically high training tempos.[19] Forward-deployed aircraft carriers and many surface combatants carry organic ASW helicopters, and carrier battle groups typically include two attack submarines.

Counters for Sea Mining. Although the Navy has robust MCM capabilities in its surface and naval aviation communities, these currently are available only in relatively limited numbers.[20] The

---

[18] Improving dedicated U.S. Navy MCM capabilities and Navy efforts to improve the organic MCM capabilities of surface vessels, suggested that the Navy's ability to deal with this threat is already good and improving. Unless they are escorted by such vessels, however, sealift ships may remain vulnerable to this threat.

[19] The naval aviation community includes both shipboard platforms, such as SH-2, SH-3, and SH-60 ASW helicopters, and land-based P-3 maritime patrol aircraft.

[20] As of 2002, the Navy has three squadrons of MCM ships, including 14 *Avenger-* and 12 *Osprey*-class ships; airborne MCM is provided for by two squadrons of 43 MH-53 Sea Dragon helicopters.

Navy also appears to be planning to increase the organic MCM capabilities of its ships, however, thus potentially reducing its need to rely on dedicated MCM ships. The net result of these two diverging trends in naval MCM capabilities seems indeterminate at present. Nevertheless, the typical concept would be for Navy MCM assets to clear mined waters and for Navy ships to escort sealifters into port. An alternative concept would be to enhance the capabilities of LMSRs and other sealift ships to detect potentially dangerous sea mines that might be avoided, or even to conduct airborne MCM operations from the decks of sealift ships. Even better would be to persuade key U.S. partners and allies in potential flashpoints (e.g., Taiwan, the Baltic states, Kuwait) to develop more robust MCM capabilities of their own.

Wild-Card Capabilities

In the course of our games, we also considered the potential role of a number of unconventional and exotic means of furthering an adversary anti-access strategy. In many cases, we judged that these sorts of capabilities were beyond the grasp of our postulated adversaries, but, if they could field such capabilities, they might play an important anti-access role. In other cases, although it was impossible to gauge the impacts of their employment, it was clear that there was more than a passing possibility that they could constitute important arrows in a future adversary's anti-access quiver.

The wild-card capabilities we considered included terrorism and SOF attacks, IO and PSYOPS, WMD (and weapons of mass disruption), EW, and computer network attacks.

Terrorism and SOF Attacks. After the attacks of September 11, the prospects for future terrorist or SOF attacks on the United States became much more imaginable for many. Equally important, the attack on the Pentagon and an apparently aborted attack on Camp David or the White House made clear that U.S. civilian and military leaders and headquarters were potential elements of the target set.

Terrorist organizations with global reach are of greatest concern.[21] Thus, until its complete elimination, al Qaeda (or its remnants) remains at the top of the list of threats to the United States.[22] However, the emergence—or resurgence—of other global terrorist organizations also would be of concern.[23] Although many regional terrorist groups seem to have little interest in attacking U.S. targets, others could pose a threat to U.S. forces and the facilities they need.[24] SOF attacks also are worrisome within a theater of operation.[25]

The same generally holds true for adversaries' intelligence and special operations capabilities for sabotage and other activities. Unlike the Soviet-era *Spetznaz* and KGB, which appeared to have something approximating global reach, at present, most nations' intelligence and special operations entities generally lack the level of organization and resources, and therefore the capabilities, to extend their reach much beyond their own regions.[26] There are, of course, exceptions,[27] and a

---

[21] Good examples of terrorist organizations that tend to restrict their operations to their own neighborhoods are the Liberation Tigers of Tamil Eelam in Sri Lanka, the al Aqsa brigade of Arafat's Fatah organization in Israel and Palestine, the Basque separatist organization ETA, and the Irish Republican Army.

[22] In his annual testimony on threats to the United States, Central Intelligence Agency Director George Tenet warned twice—on February 2, 2000, and February 7, 2001—that al Qaeda constituted the most immediate and serious threat to the nation.

[23] For example, the Japanese millenarian group Aum Shinrikyo remains both dedicated to its apocalyptic aims and well-resourced.

[24] For example, with counterdrug operations apparently increasing in the Andes region, it may be that narcoterrorist groups in Colombia and its neighbors increasingly target U.S. interests, including bases used by U.S. forces. Although the organization may have been mortally wounded by the encounter, there seems to be little doubt that U.S. support to the Filipino Army's operations against the Abu Sayyaf organization in the Philippines has earned its enmity.

[25] Bowie (2002, p. iv) reports that since 1942 there have been 645 separate attacks on airfields worldwide by special operations forces. See also Alan Vick, *Snakes in the Eagle's Nest: A History of Ground Attacks on Air Bases*, Santa Monica, Calif.: RAND Corporation, MR-553-AF, 1995.

[26] For example, North Korean special operations activities generally appear to be concentrated on South Korea.

[27] For example, Iranian intelligence continues to operate outside of the Gulf region, especially in Europe, and in concert with terrorist organizations like Lebanon's Hezbollah (Party of God).

well-resourced adversary could, with enough time, build more substantial capabilities in this area. The relative low density of likely SOF targets (e.g., LMSRs) would make them high-payoff targets for an adversary.

Of course, the counters to intelligence, special operations, and terrorist capabilities include persistent ISR, intelligence, special operations, and military police personnel, and selective hardening and other force protection activities.

IO and PSYOPS. In our scenarios, we found a potentially important role for IO and PSYOPS in sympathy with adversary anti-access strategies. Although we judged the effectiveness to be highly context-dependent, IO/PSYOPS appeared to be an important wild card, particularly in our Iraq scenario.

The principal counters to IO and PSYOPS are effective public diplomacy activities that are well-integrated into and can help to explain to foreign mass audiences diplomatic, economic, and military activities.[28] A crucial element in this is persuading partners and allies that statements by their leadership are a critical component of any such campaign because U.S. voices may be viewed as self-serving. No matter how well explained, however, high-salience U.S. policies that are viewed as fundamentally anathema by broad swaths of a region's population—e.g., U.S. support for Israel in the Arab world—are likely to eclipse such efforts. Other cultural, scientific and educational, and military activities also may help counter disaffection among elite segments of the population.

WMD (and Weapons of Mass Disruption). Another wild card is to be found in chemical, biological, radiological, nuclear, and high explosive (CBRNE) WMD—or weapons of mass *disruption*.

Our judgment was that, with the proper detection, warning, and self-protection procedures and gear, the direct military impact of chemical and biological weapon attacks could be greatly mitigated. Nevertheless, their employment might still result in mass disruption—temporary disruption or cessation of operations at targeted

---

[28] Of course, the far more diffuse commercial channels for entertainment, cultural, and other intercourse may be even more important in winning hearts and minds abroad.

bases or other facilities resulting from psychological or procedural reactions to attacks, for example, or hysteria among indigenous airfield or port workers, or mass populations. Although—or perhaps because—uncertainties remain about precisely what forms they may take, the next generation of chemical and biological weapons also offers reasons for concern. Fourth-generation chemical and biological weapons, including recombinant DNA-based "designer" bioagents immune to conventional vaccines and therapeutics, are not beyond the realm of possibility.[29]

We generally viewed radiological weapons as weapons of mass disruption—their impacts seem likely to be limited in time and space, and their employment most likely to yield psychological or procedural reactions incommensurate with their immediate lethality, including, again, the possibility for panic among mass populations.[30] Nevertheless, they could render parts of airfields or other targets unusable until they can be scrubbed of radiological detritus and thereby reduce the flow of forces.

Nuclear weapons in small numbers, whether purloined systems or improvised nuclear devices (INDs), struck us as weapons that were most likely to be withheld by a regime, both for use in coercion and bargaining in crisis and war and as the ultimate guarantor of the

---

[29] As John C. Gannon, chairman of the National Intelligence Council put it: "To add to the threat, a growing number of bad actors can choose from a widening array of new agents and new delivery systems. BCW [biological and chemical warfare] agents, as many of you know, are becoming more sophisticated and more effective. Rapid advances in biotechnology will yield new toxins or live agents, such as exotic animal viruses, that will require new detection methods and vaccines as well as other preventative measures. We are also concerned that some states might acquire more advanced and effective chemical agents, such as Russia's fourth-generation 'Novichok' agents, which are more deadly and more persistent. Gains in genetic engineering and 'designer drug'-type chemical agents are making it increasingly difficult for us to recognize all the agents threatening us" (remarks of National Intelligence Council Chairman John C. Gannon at the Hoover Institution Conference on Biological and Chemical Weapons, November 16, 1998). See also National Intelligence Council (NIC), *The Global Infectious Disease Threat and Its Implications for the United States*, Washington, D.C., NIE 99-17D, January 2000; NIC, *Global Trends 2015: A Dialogue About the Future with Nongovernment Experts*, Washington, D.C., NIC 2000-02, December 2000.

[30] This is not to say that long-term health risks would not result, just that such attacks would not typically result in large numbers of immediate radiation deaths.

regime's own survival.[31] Thus, we judged that nuclear weapons were less likely to be used against airfields, seaports, and U.S. forces in an operational or tactical role than in a strategic role. That said, we had great difficulties judging whether nuclear weapons would be most likely to be employed in the final days of a regime or would be withheld for use as a "poison pill" even after the fall of the regime, delivered, for example, by SOF or a contracted terrorist group against a large U.S. city. Adversaries with a somewhat larger inventory of nuclear weapons—even a modest nuclear force—might confer an ability to use nuclear weapons in tactical, operational, *and* strategic roles and might lead to a greater willingness to use these weapons early in a conflict.

The best counters for WMD and weapons of mass disruption in small numbers are robust capabilities for detecting, finding, targeting, and destroying them in situ or seizing and rendering them safe before they can be employed. A variety of means are available for attacking WMD facilities and stockpiles, including strike operations and direct action by SOF, although the effectiveness of these approaches seems somewhat doubtful. Failing prevention, shelters and other hardening and robust force protection and reconstitution capabilities are needed to mitigate the consequences of WMD events, although again, hardening is unlikely to be very effective against nuclear attack.

The study team judged that the United States probably would respond very differently to potential adversaries with large inventories of nuclear weapons, and would impose constraints on military elements of its counter strategy for ensuring access to avoid escalation to a nuclear exchange. Additionally, the historical reliance on deterrence and assured destruction would remain the policy of choice for keeping operations below the nuclear threshold.

EW. Our study did not explore in depth the technological feasibility or likely performance characteristics of next-generation EW capabilities, much less possible operational concepts for their employ-

---

[31] This seemed likely because nuclear weapons are systems whose use would represent a significant escalation in a crisis or war and would potentially invite a U.S. response that was comparable in consequence if not in kind.

ment. Nevertheless, we viewed with some concern the apparent trends in EW capabilities, including GPS and other jamming capabilities, jam-resistant guidance systems, and a range of other possible electronic exotica, including radio frequency (RF), electromagnetic pulse (EMP), laser, and microwave weapons.

Our judgment was that Russia seems likely to retain a substantial R&D capability for the maturation of these technologies. This, coupled with its continued substantial presence in the global arms market as a means for increasing its hard currency and trade position, suggests that Russia may be a major proliferator of any operational capabilities that actually may emerge from research in these areas. The PRC also has expressed great interest in advanced EW capabilities to help underwrite its concept of "high-tech war under local conditions" and accordingly also should be monitored.

Because of the plethora of technical details involved, and the likelihood that effective implementations using these technologies might not emerge for a decade or longer, identifying counters in this area proved impossible. It is nevertheless an area that needs to be closely monitored by the Army and other intelligence organizations.

Cyber Warfare. Another wild card that also proved difficult to assess was the potential payoff of computer network attacks and other forms of cyber warfare in support of adversary anti-access strategies. The PRC, Russia, and many other states appear to have—or are developing—incipient cyber warfare capabilities that might be employed against in-theater, en-route, or CONUS-based information and communication systems.

The best course of action is to ensure that mission-critical systems and networks—including logistics and sustainment systems—are not accessible through the Internet, where they are at heightened risk of attack. The next step is to create mutually reinforcing and complementary layered defenses. Effective personnel security programs and password security are critical to mitigate the threat from insiders with access. System administrators need to ensure that computers and networks are promptly updated with newly available software patches that plug known holes in security. Capabilities for quick detection and containment or other responses to computer network intrusions, viruses, and other forms of attack need to be established at all levels, including desktop computers, network servers, firewalls, and switchers.[32] Finally, capabilities for identifying and tracking malefactors and targeting attacking systems for counterattack should be developed, although it may be exceedingly difficult to do this fast enough to help put attacks in context.

We conclude this chapter by reemphasizing that potential weapon systems need to be considered in a larger technological and organizational milieu and not as stand-alone systems. Thus, it also will be important for the Army and other intelligence organizations to monitor the emergence of new operational concepts and doctrine and to track prototyping and experimentation, readiness, training and exercises, organizational, and other "soft" factors because more capability may arise from the more clever assemblage and use of existing systems.

---

[32] Some advantages also may be gained by diversifying the combinations of desktop computers, servers, firewalls, and switches, insofar as each presents a different set of hacking problems, and more randomness in the assembly of different options makes each target less predictable (and less hackable).

CHAPTER EIGHT

Toward a Strategy for Assuring Access

As described in Chapter Two, the study team came to view the question of access as a long-term game in which the United States and its potential regional adversaries sought, in peacetime, crisis, and conflict, to shape the future U.S. access environment.

As we came to better understand the access game through our scenario gaming, the outlines of an access strategy began to emerge. This strategy is deliberate and long term in nature; is comprised of peacetime, crisis, and conflict activities; and embraces both the principles of trial and error and graceful failure modes discussed in Chapter Two (see Figure 8.1). Importantly, peacetime preparation and contingency planning are essential to deal with access challenges. If done properly, these challenges need not be a major problem if a crisis actually does occur.

During peacetime, the U.S. aims are threefold: enhancing regional security and stability by assuring partners and allies while deterring adversaries and maintaining and developing new options. These options are of two kinds. The first is expanding the portfolio of available bases and other infrastructure that might be needed to conduct military operations—e.g., through a range of formal and informal arrangements and understandings.[1] It includes improving U.S.

---

[1] Our view on this is consistent with Bowie's (2002, p. v) recommendation that the United States "engage as wide an array of nations as possible to increase the chances of obtaining access when needed. Nonetheless, history illustrates that the unpredictability of the location

Figure 8.1
A Strategy for Assuring Access

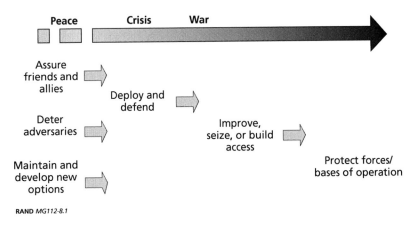

RAND MG112-8.1

military capabilities (both combat and mobility) in ways that make U.S. forces less vulnerable to anti-access strategies—e.g., by reducing their need for mature basing and infrastructure, enhancing their self-deployability, and enhancing capabilities for the assault, seizure, and improvement of airfields, seaports, and other infrastructure.[2]

During crisis or war, U.S. forces will deploy and defend the airfields, seaports, and bases they will need to ensure a smooth buildup of forces, as well as protecting U.S. and coalition forces themselves. They also will defend leadership and population targets that an adversary might threaten to drive political wedges between the United

---

and nature of future conflicts will make it difficult to forecast the attitude of host countr[ies] when access is needed." He further recommends infrastructure development, including base development and prepositioning; dispersal; suppressing anti-access threats rapidly; large, man-made islands; active defenses; and bases outside the range of threat systems. See also Paul Killingsworth et al., *Flexbasing: Achieving Global Presence for Expeditionary Aerospace Forces,* Santa Monica, Calif.: RAND Corporation, MR-1113-AF, 2000.

[2] Our view is consistent with Coté's (2000) position that "the need to avoid or reduce dependence on assured access to [fixed] bases ashore is the one common link between the near and more distant security environments that can be seen clearly today, and it is therefore the dominant measure of effectiveness that U.S. political and military leaders should use in fashioning their military forces to meet the demands of the new security environment. In responding to this imperative, they will need to find ways of making land-based forces less dependent on fixed bases, and of assuring that naval forces can simultaneously maintain access to the sea and project more power from it."

States and its partners and allies or to coerce regional partners and allies into withholding or reducing needed access. If suitable airfields or ports are unavailable, the United States either can improve more austere bases that remain available, seize and improve bases that meet its needs (e.g., on the adversary's own territory), or build new (albeit probably bare-bones) bases.[3] Finally, the strategy envisages U.S. forces protecting forces and bases of operation until the operation is concluded or even after, if a postconflict U.S. presence is needed.

We now discuss some of the ways and means associated with each element of this strategy. We conclude the chapter with a discussion of the implications for the SBCT and Objective Force BCT, and for joint modernization and transformation efforts.

Peacetime Activities

The new strategy promoted in the most recent Quadrennial Defense Review includes as two of its principal objectives the aims of "assuring friends and allies" and "deterring potential adversaries."[4] We believe that both of these aims also promote access.[5]

---

[3] Of course, to the extent that peacetime efforts to reduce U.S. forces' needs for very mature basing are successful, it may be possible in many cases to conduct operations out of more austere bases with a minimal level of improvement. Bowie (2002, pp. 20–22) shows that building new bases during a conflict has been a fairly common enterprise and notes that USAF stood up 13 new airfields in and around Afghanistan during the recent operations.

[4] Department of Defense, *Quadrennial Defense Review Report*, Washington, D.C., September 30, 2001.

[5] What follows seems consistent with a review in Shlapak et al. (2002) of the history of U.S. access, which identified six factors associated with cooperation, including access. The three factors that favored cooperation were close alignment and sustained military connections, shared interests and objectives, and hopes for closer ties with the United States. Factors working against cooperation were fear of reprisals, conflicting goals and interests, and domestic public opinion. See Shlapak et al. (2002, p. xv). For another excellent historical review of the access and basing problem with an accent on the Air Force, see Bowie (2002).

Assuring Partners and Allies

Partners and allies will be assured to the extent that the United States has military capabilities that are likely to prove decisive in influencing the outcome of a crisis or conflict and that U.S. security guarantees of support in crisis or war are viewed as credible. That assurance rests only in part on perceptions of U.S. military prowess and the credibility of U.S. security guarantees in the face of external threats.

Many regional partners and allies also face internal threats to their security, and adversaries may seek to influence their behavior—or depose them—by providing symbolic or material resources to opposition forces, sleeper cells, and the like.[6] When faced both with internal and external threats to their security, regional partners and allies will calculate whether the status quo relationship with the United States enhances their overall security. If the status quo arrangement is viewed as failing to enhance overall security, actions may be taken—either toward a closer or more distant relationship with the United States—that can better realize the desired level of security.

In making this calculation, partners and allies will assess the likelihood of war, the regional correlation of forces in such a war, how that correlation might shift given U.S. military involvement in a broader war, and whether U.S. involvement is in fact likely. But they also will assess the impact on the threats and risks posed by core constituencies within their own populations of various forms of cooperation with the United States, and the extent to which the overall alignment of U.S. interests and preferences on key security and other issues ultimately enhances or reduces their security from internal threats.

---

[6] In its weakest form, this may simply take the shape of opposition groups that follow the rules of competition in a democratic political society. In its strongest form, it may take the shape of opposition groups that seek the extraconstitutional overthrow of a regime and therefore may pose an existential threat not just to the regime but to the constitutional framework of which it is an expression. We here emphasize the violent and extraconstitutional variant, not the democratic one, because the United States can or will do little to affect internal political balances.

To the extent that allies conclude that their overall security interests are best served by a closer relationship with the United States, additional cooperation of various kinds can be expected, including plans to provide access to U.S. forces under various circumstances.[7] To the extent that the relationship with the United States is increasingly seen as a liability, cooperation might be reduced.[8] Thus, the antecedent for increased security cooperation—including access—will be some degree of harmonization in threat perceptions and in calculations of which policies and positions will best enhance overall security in the face of external and internal threats.[9] In many cases, however, this will prove impossible, as when the United States is effectively asked to abandon a friend or ally (e.g., Israel) or make a significant change to a core security policy.

Deterring Adversaries

For many of the same reasons, potential adversaries will be deterred to the extent that they believe that the likely payoffs of efforts to forcibly change the status quo are less than those associated with its continuation.[10] In this, to the extent that the regional correlation of military capabilities—including the potential contributions of extra-regional actors, such as the United States, and the reliability of the U.S. security commitment—do not favor them, they are likely to be

---

[7] For example, Taiwan has concluded that its security is enhanced by security cooperation with the United States.

[8] For example, key regional partners, such as Saudi Arabia (and South Korea), can face a difficult trade-off in calibrating their desired level of cooperation with the United States. Although cooperation may enhance security against such external threats as Iraq (or North Korea), it does so at an increasing cost in terms of reducing security against internal threats (e.g., a backlash from an increasingly unhappy Arab street or a somewhat restive South Korean electorate).

[9] It goes without saying that one way that U.S. partners have finessed these sorts of issues is to have a more distant public posture with the United States, while privately providing assurances and engaging in other forms of cooperation.

[10] For complementary views of deterrence calculations, see Alexander L. George and Richard Smoke, *Deterrence in American Foreign Policy*, New York: Columbia University Press, 1974; Bruce Bueno de Mesquita, *Principles of International Politics*, Washington, D.C.: Congressional Quarterly Press, 2000.

deterred or to fall back on less direct means for shaping events in ways that can assist them in realizing their objectives without triggering a U.S. military response. To the extent that adversaries calculate (or miscalculate) that they can prevail at an acceptable cost, however, they are unlikely to be deterred.

Predicated on this understanding of assurance and deterrence, a wide range of activities can further promote the objective of assuring allies and partners and improving the prospects for access.

As was discussed in Chapters Three through Six, many of these activities already are conducted under the umbrella of each regional commander's theater security cooperation plan, including Army international activities. These activities include a rich array of exchanges, training and education, exercises, conferences, planning, and other measures that can lead to deeper understanding and fostering areas of common interest and are supplemented by sales of selected systems that can enhance compatibility and interoperability.[11] The credibility of U.S. security guarantees can also be emphasized through measures that enhance the effectiveness of combat capabilities and their responsiveness, deployability, and sustainability. These will be discussed next.

Maintaining and Developing New Options

In addition to actions to assure and deter, the broader access strategy is underwritten by a range of largely peacetime U.S. efforts that aim to diversify the portfolio of basing options in each theater and improve the access-enhancing characteristics of U.S. forces.

Diversifying the Portfolio of Basing Options. Part of the purpose for the current study was to identify worldwide access "requirements" for Army land forces. As we studied the adversary anti-access problem, however, we soon learned two things.

---

[11] For a conceptual framework for considering the interoperability problem and its application to coalition air operations, see Myron Hura et al., *Interoperability: A Continuing Challenge in Coalition Air Operations*, Santa Monica, Calif.: RAND Corporation, MR-1235-AF, 2000.

First, actual access needs vary greatly in kind and magnitude depending on the mission, the size of the operation, the specific composition of the forces, and a host of other variables. Rather than the small number of cases we were able to examine, literally hundreds of cases would need to be assessed to establish access requirements (e.g., "best" alternatives, "second-best" alternatives, and so on) for each of the potential permutations.

Second, the basing and other host nation support that might be made available in any given scenario also would hinge on the characteristics of each case, and it was very easy for us to imagine different scenarios in which the same countries offered—or withheld—access, depending on the specific configuration of variables. These variables could include the identity of the adversary, the extent to which regional partners shared the U.S. threat perceptions and beliefs about the importance and urgency of a military response, the overall correlation between U.S. and friendly nations' security policies, and specific regional dynamics.

As we considered these issues, the basing aspects of the access issue increasingly seemed to pivot on the question of how large and well-diversified the portfolio of available access options might be at any given time, and whether, over time, the number of options and the overall diversification of the portfolio were increasing or decreasing. The issue, it seemed, was not fixed or enduring "requirements" but rather whether the portfolio of basing options offered a growing number of viable fallbacks in any given case—a range of suitable alternatives that might support the mission. The aim should be to assess the range of alternatives available in a theater and foster arrangements for access under a range of circumstances.[12]

Although a full discussion of the issue was beyond the scope of this report and could constitute a study in its own right, balancing such a portfolio could require diversifying across a rather large num-

_____

[12] A separately published appendix provides a crude prioritization of worldwide airfields and seaports that can serve as a basis for maintaining and enhancing the portfolio of basing alternatives. Airfields are categorized as primary (preferred) airfields or secondary (second-best) or tertiary (third-best) fallback options. We also identify worldwide LMSR-capable large ports.

ber of dimensions. These dimensions include land- and sea-based basing options,[13] basing in multiple countries to avoid an undue reliance on single points of failure (e.g., a single country's hospitality), alternative transportation modes (e.g., air, sea, or land), bases that vary in their distance from the likely combat zone (e.g., a mix of theater forward operating bases and other bases), bases that vary in their level of maturity and sophistication, bases that can be used both for permissive and forced entry into a theater, and so on.

Improving the Access-Enhancing Characteristics of U.S. Forces. The second activity is to develop new aims to shape future U.S. forces—mobility, combat, combat support, and combat service support—in ways that can improve the access-enhancing characteristics of these forces and thereby reduce their vulnerability to adversary anti-access strategies.

DoD should consider pursuing a range of options that would further diversify and enhance the U.S. portfolio of mobility capabilities while enhancing flexibility by reducing their requirements for mature infrastructure; improve the deployability and self-deployability of some forces to underwrite new deployment and warfighting concepts; and ensure capabilities for rapidly assaulting, seizing, and securing objectives and providing necessary force protection. DoD should also consider options that would ensure capabilities for improvement or construction of expeditionary bases so they might be used to receive forces and be made suitable bases of operation.

Diversifying and Enhancing the Flexibility of Mobility Capabilities. A richer set of options for deploying forces will likely be more difficult for an adversary to successfully counter than a more limited set. In addition, the more flexible mobility capabilities are, the greater the likelihood that the United States can expeditiously deploy and employ forces, even in less well-developed theaters.

- *Air Mobility.* The emergence of forward operating bases—air bases on the periphery of the theater and out of range of missiles

---

[13] For example, for a number of years large sea bases have been considered as an alternative to land-based airfields.

and other adversary anti-access capabilities—for airlift operations offers interesting possibilities for underwriting new deployment and employment concepts. For example, ground forces might be moved by strategic lift to the forward operating bases and then by theater airlifters (e.g., C-130s) directly to relatively unimproved airstrips in the combat zone, where they could conduct dispersed and nonlinear operations. Thus, a mix of strategic and theater airlifters in the mobility force structure might underwrite entirely new concepts for more dispersed and nonlinear operations by ground forces, while reducing the vulnerability of inventory-limited C-5s and C-17s.[14]

- *Sea Mobility*. Sea-based mobility capabilities that bear further consideration include high-speed, shallow-draft sealift, improved lighterage, sea bases, and even such unconventional concepts as dirigibles that might substitute for lighterage and be used in cases where mature seaports are unavailable.

- *Prepositioning*. Expanded prepositioning also can foster greater diversification. Land-based prepositioning limits mobility needs to the airlift of personnel, while in-theater, sea-based prepositioning can greatly reduce the amount of time that would have been needed to deploy an equivalent set of unit equipment from CONUS. Sea-based prepositioning is also potentially less vulnerable to anti-access attacks than fixed, land-based prepositioning sites.

Enhancing Deployability and Self-Deployability. By reducing the volumetrics (cubic size and weight) of unit equipment to be airlifted, Army forces might either be deployed in a smaller number of strategic airlift missions, or be deployed in-theater by more plentiful C-130s.[15] Reducing the size and weight of missile defenses may

---

[14] This can, of course, create serious challenges for logistics personnel who must sustain dispersed operations.

[15] A concept that relied more heavily on C-5s and C-17s to bring forces to peripheral airfields and then deployed them within the theater by C-130 also would increase the number of in-theater airfields that could be used for the final leg of the deployment. To accomplish

similarly facilitate their speedy deployment, thereby enhancing the security of early-arriving forces by neutralizing air and missile threats. Likewise, efforts to improve the threat detection and self-protection capabilities of mobility forces may reduce their vulnerability to anti-access attacks. For example, improved flares, chaff, electronic, and other self-protection means can be developed for airlifters, and mine detection and MCM or ASW capabilities might be deployed on board sealift ships.

Moreover, improving the self-deployability of certain assets, such as attack helicopters, might enable new deployment and employment concepts: attack helicopters might be strategically lifted to locations on the periphery of a theater and then self-deploy into the combat zone, reducing at least somewhat their overall mobility needs, or, rather than being concentrated, they might operate from dispersed locations that could be concealed from the adversary.

Ensuring Assault, Forced-Entry, Seizure, and Force Protection Capabilities. In some instances—that is, where needed bases are unavailable—theater access may require seizing and protecting the infrastructure needed to receive U.S. forces. This has two main consequences for planning.

To protect forces and bases of operation, what will be needed is a rapidly deployable joint capability to seize, hold, and control a three-dimensional space—air, land, and sea—and keep it substantially free of threats until it is no longer needed.[16] This three-dimensional space could be a small area, where a temporary sanctuary is created for U.S. or coalition forces, or it could include large swaths of the theater of interest.[17] In anti-access and area-denial environ-

---

this, however, new concepts for speedy reloading of cargo from strategic to theater airlifters would be needed.

[16] The no-fly zones in Bosnia and southern and northern Iraq, the unsuccessful "United Nations Safe Areas" imposed in Srebrenica, and no-movement zones created in southern Iraq after the Gulf War, maritime interception zones, and layered theater missile defenses all are examples of such a concept.

[17] This concept is an extension of the "defense bubble for air and missile defense" proposed by General James P. McCarthy, USAF (Ret.). See DoD, "Special DoD News Briefing on Defense Transformation," June 12, 2001.

ments, force and base protection capabilities will be needed from the time the first U.S. forces arrive in theater until they depart. Protecting bases of operation also may include protecting regional leaders and populations from external and internal threats.[18] Thus a range of forced-entry or assault; air defense; nuclear, biological, and chemical (NBC) protection; and other force protection and engineering capabilities may be needed.

First, efforts should be made to develop or refine the needed CONOPs and joint doctrine to ensure robust capabilities for the successful seizure of air bases, seaports, and other needed infrastructure and to provide robust force protection for early-entry forces. Reconnaissance, strike, engineer, and other operations may need to precede or accompany forced-entry operations by airborne and amphibious assault forces that have the mission of seizing air bases, seaports, or other needed infrastructure that can provide a lodgment for force buildups. While these forces seize and secure new bases of operation, they need to be protected from efforts to dislodge them through strikes, counterassaults, and other means. Early-entry forces' protection needs seem likely to include persistent ISR, perimeter security, and missile defense capabilities but could include other capabilities.[19]

Second, campaign planning will need to consider the possibility that, in cases where bases are either inadequate or unavailable, airfields, seaports, and other infrastructure may need to be seized in an operation's early phases. Operational plans should therefore be modified to include branches and sequels that envision such activities.

Enhancing Expeditionary Engineering Capabilities for Infrastructure Improvement and Construction. Finally, ensuring access may require additional, highly expeditionary capabilities for improving immature infrastructure or, in cases where no infrastructure

---

[18] See for example, Tony Perry, "Fear and Loathing in Kuwait," *Los Angeles Times*, September 30, 2002, p. A1.

[19] When needed infrastructure is in or adjacent to urban areas, adversaries may engage in attacks on bases in an effort draw forces into urban terrain where they may be more vulnerable to attack. Thus, force protection also could include armored and mechanized forces supporting dismounted infantry.

exists, constructing new infrastructure foundations literally from the ground up.[20] A wide range of capabilities and units—Army Combat Engineer and Force Provider units, Air Force RED HORSE squadrons and Harvest Falcon bare base sets, Naval Construction Battalions, and so on—theoretically could help underwrite joint expeditionary improvement and construction concepts that could expand the range of bases and infrastructure that meet minimal standards for deployment or other operations.[21]

Investments in Self-Defense by U.S. Partners and Allies

Before turning to the crisis and wartime elements of the strategy, it is worth noting that many of these areas also can benefit greatly from investments that U.S. allies themselves make to improve their self-defense capabilities and the access outlook for the United States. Among these investments are air and missile defenses, MCM and ASW, construction of new airfields, port facilities, and other infrastructure, hardening of C2 and access-related infrastructure, and a variety of other means. In the end, to the extent that partners and allies can provide for their own defense, the needed commitment of forces from the United States—and U.S. access needs—will be reduced. DoD planners need to consider the question of how best to give incentives for such efforts by allies and partners.[22]

Crisis and Wartime Activities

Returning to Figure 8.1, the strategy for ensuring access envisions that the sorts of capabilities just described can help to underwrite three additional tasks: deploying and defending forces; improving,

---

[20] To the extent that efforts to reduce the infrastructure requirements of mobility and combat forces are successful, this will reduce the difficulty of these tasks.

[21] Unfortunately, these units are all very heavy and therefore require substantial lift themselves.

[22] For example, expansion of available infrastructure might be scored in the annual DoD effort to assess allied contributions to the common defense.

seizing, or building access; and protecting forces and bases of operation.

Because these three tasks were described in some detail above, here we simply highlight some additional top-level points for Army consideration.

Deploying and Defending

As the Army develops its SBCT and Objective Force BCT and as it considers concepts for deployment of forces directly into the combat zone, it will also need to wrestle with the full range of supporting capabilities that may be needed but may not be organic to these units.

In some scenarios, forced-entry or assault forces (e.g., Rangers, airborne) may first be needed to seize and then secure infrastructure before additional units can be deployed into the combat zone. Persistent ISR, air and missile defenses, and other force protection capabilities, as well as deep-strike and other combat capabilities all may be needed by these units in many easily imagined scenarios. Operations in urban areas may prove to be particularly challenging because urban canyons can limit both ISR and mobility and urban adversaries can integrate better off-the-shelf communications technology—or even nontechnological approaches[23]—with command-and-control arrangements that can enable "swarming" and other tactics to place arriving U.S. forces at risk.[24] Put another way, the Army will need to consider the shape (and deployment needs) of a potentially wide range of capabilities while working within the joint community to ensure that the requisite airlift or other mobility resources will be made available.

Improving, Seizing, or Building Access

In spite of peacetime efforts to enhance available basing options, in crisis or conflict the United States may still face significant restric-

---

[23] For example, the Somalis' doctrine was simply to "run to the smoke" of a downed helicopter, which required nothing in the way of technology.

[24] For an excellent treatment of how adversaries can adapt highly effective operational concepts in urban warfighting, see Mark Bowden, *Black Hawk Down: A Story of Modern Warfare*, New York: Signet Books, 1999.

tions on its regional access. In such circumstances, three basic options are available: the United States may seek to improve existing facilities to the point where they will be serviceable; it may seize facilities and, if necessary, improve those; or it may build new facilities.

As discussed above, these sorts of construction activities require somewhat specialized combat support capabilities that typically reside in units that are available in only small numbers in the current force structure.[25] Some of these capabilities, moreover—the sorts of combat engineering capabilities that would be needed to improve or build new facilities is a good example—can be rather large in terms of unit weight and also can require heavy and bulky materials (e.g., sand, concrete, water) to accomplish their mission. They would therefore need to compete for scarce mobility resources. As a design point, the Army and joint community need to continue and expand their existing efforts regarding operational concepts suitable for the sorts of activities that may be needed to ensure access in a crisis or conflict and actions that can give these forces the expeditionary characteristics of responsiveness and low weight.

Protecting Forces and Bases of Operation

All other things being equal, the geographic proximity of potential regional adversaries to U.S. partners and allies may provide them with multiple potential axes for attacking access-related targets and arriving U.S. forces. The distinct preference of the United States—or better put, its need—for mature and capable airfields, seaports, and other infrastructure can make it even easier for the adversary to guess where best to concentrate its efforts. In the face of these adversary advantages, concepts that can protect forces and bases of operation— potentially including regional leaders and populations—are needed from the beginning of a crisis through the duration of a campaign.

---

[25] Airfield seizure can be done, for example, by Army Rangers, Airborne units, or Marines.

The Question of Costs

It is important to note that many of the activities to ensure access suggested by our strategy are likely to prove extremely costly. The cost of base development in current-year dollars recently was estimated at about $30 billion, and hardening European air bases was even more costly; the cost of a single Joint Mobile Offshore Base has been estimated at $6 billion; and dispersal of forces and operations likely will be expensive to support.[26] The cost of layered theater missile defenses and those for high-speed sealift, lighterage, floating docks, airlifters, prepositioning, and other access-enhancing efforts are likely to be similarly expensive. It will, accordingly, be extremely important to consider various options in the context of a much broader trade space.

In the next chapter, we describe implications for the Army and joint community and offer our concluding observations.

---

[26] Cost estimates from Bowie (2002, pp. v–vi).

CHAPTER NINE

Conclusions and Implications

As described in the preceding chapters, the anti-access threat generally appears to be manageable in the short term but sufficiently serious to justify both more detailed analysis and serious policy consideration. For as this report has shown, while adversary anti-access options and potential U.S. counters can only be truly understood in the context of specific theaters, adversaries, and campaigns, there are many moving parts to the anti-access problem, which in turn dictates an overarching, integrated strategy for ensuring future U.S. access in critical regions.

We now turn to the implications of this research for intelligence and transformation activities and the contributions that they might make to an overall access strategy.

Implications for Intelligence Needs

The emerging anti-access environment and the long-term strategy for assuring access will accent both strategic and technical intelligence collection and analysis. Each will be discussed briefly.

Strategic Intelligence

The question of access in any given contingency (or theater) hinges on a range of strategic-level issues that need to be followed very closely by military and civilian intelligence personnel. Among the strategic-level collection and analysis areas of increasing importance from an access perspective that are related to potential adversaries are the following:

- Overt and covert efforts to influence, bribe, or coerce U.S. partners and allies to distance themselves from the United States.[1]
- Defense spending intentions and priorities, especially with respect to choices made regarding a reliance on advanced technologies or more conventional ones, and on capabilities that can be used to underwrite anti-access strategies.
- National armaments policies, especially relating to choices between indigenous production and acquisition abroad and to the level of integration of military and civilian R&D and industrial bases.[2]

Among the collection areas of increasing importance related to U.S. partners and allies are the following:

- General trends in leadership, elite, and population attitudes toward or away from the United States.
- Leadership perceptions of their security situations, especially whether they view the principal threats to their security as internal or external, and the perceived role of the United States in exacerbating or mitigating these threats.
- The actual level of success that potential U.S. adversaries seem to be having in making inroads with U.S. partners and allies whose assistance may be crucial to success in a campaign.
- Internal political pressures and unrest regarding relations with the United States.

---

[1]For example, in the recent run-up to what was in fall 2002 widely expected to be a war with Iraq, it sought to bribe U.S. partners and allies, among others, through lucrative contracts. See Evelyn Iritani, "Iraq Fights Back with Commerce," *Los Angeles Times*, November 11, 2002. This followed on the heels of an Iraqi "charm offensive" in which senior Iraqi leaders shuttled between Persian Gulf capitals in an effort to isolate the United States.

[2]On the possible future shape of the arms industry, see John Battilega et al., *Transformations in Global Defense Markets and Industries: Implications for the Future of Warfare*, Washington, D.C., 2000, a study supported by the National Intelligence Council.

- Defense spending intentions and priorities, especially in those areas that can best mitigate adversary anti-access threats (e.g., missile defenses, MCM, interoperability with U.S. forces, hardening).
- Investment decisions related to the construction of new ports or airfields, or the improvement or expansion of existing ones.

It will be important to ensure that intelligence information and resulting estimates on these issues are kept up-to-date, to better support the adjustment of operational plans in the actual event of an emerging crisis or contingency.

Operational Military Intelligence

A number of collection priorities also are of an operational military nature. Access-related collection priorities include monitoring potential adversaries' developments for evidence of the following:

- Investments in key areas that can shed light on the nature of the anti-access threat, including increased inventories of ballistic (especially mobile) and/or cruise missiles, nuclear weapons, improved precision coupled with C3ISR capabilities to provide more accurate, real-time targeting data, and/or area munitions, such as cluster munitions and long-range SAMs.
- An improved capability to conduct joint and combined-arms operations because this could enable new and more threatening operational concepts.
- Demonstration of new operational concepts, doctrine, and organizations that might enable new types of anti-access operations.
- Enhanced training and other efforts to improve quality in key niche areas.
- Airfields, seaports, and other infrastructure that might be seized from the adversary and used as a base of operation, as well as their characteristics and suitability for various uses.

Access-related collection priorities related to U.S. partners and allies include the following:

- Changes in qualitative performance, especially with respect to mobilization, deployment, and the conduct of combat operations.
- The evolving level of compatibility and interoperability with U.S. forces and capabilities, especially in air and missile defenses.
- The characteristics and capabilities of the inventory of ports, airfields, and other infrastructure that might be used in a deployment, their suitability for various types of operations, and judgments on the level of effort that would be required to improve or expand them to make them suitable for reception of U.S. forces or for conducting U.S. military operations.

As with the strategic-level intelligence, it will be important to stay abreast of these issues.

Technical Intelligence

We cannot know with any precision the new capabilities adversaries might be able to field between now and 2012, much less beyond 2012. In part, this involves uncertainties about nations' abilities to research, develop, and field advanced capabilities; the technological risks inherent in such efforts; choices among competing claimants for scarce resources; and numerous other factors. It also involves uncertainties with regard to the future shape of the global arms market that will, in part, regulate which capabilities get in whose hands, especially those regarding what suppliers will be willing to sell to others. Two main areas of intelligence collection and analysis will be crucial in helping to narrow these uncertainties.

First, it will be critically important to monitor the development of new operational concepts, doctrine, and organizations that could be used to complicate U.S. regional access and how changes in training and exercise levels might result in greater operational proficiency. Wealthier and technologically more advanced adversaries seem more likely to develop new concepts than do poor and technologically impoverished ones.

Second, it will be critical for intelligence organizations to continuously monitor and assess national (both military and civilian, public and private) long-range research and development efforts to identify the technologies that might underpin those future operational concepts. In addition to the capabilities we identified in Chapter Seven, among the research, development, and acquisition areas that the defense intelligence community needs to watch for are

- nuclear weapons;
- integrated C3ISR capabilities that can provide the "system of systems" needed to exploit increased precision;
- next-generation biological and chemical weapons;
- EMP or other RF technologies;
- laser technologies;
- microwave technologies;
- IO;
- EW capabilities; and
- increasingly accurate conventional or advanced supercavitation-based torpedoes or other capabilities.

Commercial Intelligence

Global defense markets are in the midst of a substantial transformation that has been characterized by increased concentration and specialization among arms producers, different national choices regarding the mix of commercial and military activities in their national armament programs, and continued diffusion of advanced-technology weapons to developing nations.[3]

The consequence is that intelligence personnel will need to closely monitor military research and development efforts and arms sales policies—especially in Russia, France, North Korea, Israel, and other nations that have demonstrated their willingness to sell advanced technologies to potential U.S. adversaries. In particular, because it has sophisticated military R&D capabilities, it will be criti-

---

[3]See Battilega et al. (2000).

cally important to closely follow what Russia seems to be developing for its own purposes, and what it is selling to others.[4]

International specialization in the commercial arms market may increasingly lead to different market leaders in specific niche areas. The implication for access-related intelligence collection and analyses is that they may in the future come to more closely resemble industry analysis.[5]

Implications for Transformation Management

Our analyses generally assumed that the Army and DoD would continue to make improvements in a number of core areas—theater air and missile defenses, forced entry, force protection, persistent ISR, and so on—that would improve the future access outlook for U.S. land forces against current anti-access threats and those that can be discerned on the horizon.

Indeed, we expect an increasing pace of technological change and diffusion of technology that could threaten the U.S. access outlook in key theaters and will challenge traditional approaches to developing new military capabilities with implications for both of the sponsors of this report:

- As described above, intelligence personnel will need to closely monitor and provide nearly continuous threat assessments of a wide range of potentially important political, military, and technological access-related developments to ensure that counters can be developed for emerging adversary anti-access strategies and capabilities in an effective and timely manner.

---

[4]The NIC's *Global Trends 2015* (2000, p. 53) notes that "[a]s Russia struggles with constraints on its ambitions, it will invest scarce resources in selected and secretive military technology programs, especially WMD, hoping to counter Western conventional and strategic superiorities in areas such as ballistic missile defense."

[5]Whether such analyses are best performed by the government or by private-sector firms that specialize in such analyses is an open issue.

- The Army G-3's ongoing efforts to plan the Army's transformation will need to ensure that the implications of emerging threats and capabilities for transformation are fully considered, and force development and research, development, test, and evaluation plans are adapted to better meet emerging threats.
- Of particular importance in this regard will be establishing a formal airlift requirement for the SBCT and Objective Force BCT. We recommend that, in addition to the brigade airdrop requirement that currently exists, a requirement be established to deploy a single Army SBCT or Objective Force BCT within a specified time line. Absent such a requirement, future brigade combat teams may have great difficulties securing the necessary lift.[6] The Army should be mindful, however, that the SBCT and Objective Force BCT likely must demonstrate substantial combat capabilities if it is to receive a larger slice of airlift resources.
- For the Army RDT&E community, the access problem seems likely to increasingly demand a philosophy of rapid prototyping, early fielding and testing, and spiral development. If true, this would have profound implications for the manner and pace of Army research, development, and acquisition.

The centerpiece of the Army's transformation effort is the transition to SBCTs and the Objective Force, and the Army has at most only two full development cycles between now and 2017, when the Objective Force combat teams will be fielded.[7]

- During the first (2003–2010) development period, the Army should concentrate on improving the SBCT's access outlook and refining its understanding of the SBCT's needs for the following sorts of capabilities: airlift, sealift, and prepositioning; air defense; sustainment; expeditionary airfield and port erection

---

[6]We also acknowledge that such a requirement might necessitate an increase in the required size of the C-17 fleet.

[7]The estimate that two full development cycles can be conducted between 2003 and 2012 is probably an exceedingly optimistic one.

and improvement; long-range fires; NBC reconnaissance, decontamination, and other force protection capabilities; and the command, control, and communications that will be required to provide the SBCT with its supporting capabilities. The Army also should be identifying new capabilities needed to respond to emerging anti-access threats.

- During the second development period, the Army should continue to focus on identifying supporting capabilities that will further improve the access outlook for SBCTs and Objective Force BCTs, even as intelligence organizations continue to identify new access-related threats.

As has been described in this report, the anti-access threat to U.S. ground forces generally seems manageable for the near term—i.e., out to about 2012—although this conclusion is accompanied by a number of important caveats, summarized at the beginning of this chapter. Beyond 2012, it seems plausible that adversary anti-access strategies may become more sophisticated and anti-access capabilities will improve, possibly in dramatic and surprising ways.

The imperatives for transformation of U.S. forces to improve their ability to deal with anti-access and area-denial environments are not just found in the emerging threat environment and the new defense strategy's high prioritization of these threats, however. They also are to be found in the realities of the service competition that will animate the future transformation of the force. As Coté (2000) has observed:

> In the more distant term, if they do not transform, major ground formations and air expeditionary forces will face serious military constraints on their ability to deploy to major contingencies because the ports and airfields that they now depend on will simply not be viable. . . . That help [in meeting the future demand for better capabilities for dealing with anti-access environments] can come either in the form of real transformation efforts by the other services, or by increased budget share for the Navy. The best way for U.S. political leaders to maximize the probability of either one of those outcomes is to formulate a

military strategy that defense spending priorities will [be based on the] primary measure of effectiveness for future military forces [of] assured access in an environment where access to bases ashore will be inherently limited. Such a strategy would either catalyze the transformation efforts that are necessary, particularly in the Army and the Air Force, or lead to the reallocation of resources that will be necessary if the Navy is to fill the void.

We believe that the work presented here identifies many of the questions of greatest concern to the Army and DoD, and provides some tentative answers to these questions. It also provides some pointers to the tenets of an integrated strategy for the Army and DoD. Nonetheless, a great deal of additional work will be needed to ensure that emerging anti-access threats to U.S. ground forces are successfully managed.

Bibliography

Books and Reports

Battilega, John, Randall Greenwalt, David Beachley, Daniel Beck, Robert Driver, and Bruce Jackson, *Transformations in Global Defense Markets and Industries: Implications for the Future of Warfare,* Washington, D.C.: National Intelligence Council, 2000.

Bennett, Bruce, Christopher P. Twomey, and Gregory F. Treverton, *What Are Asymmetric Strategies?* Santa Monica, Calif.: RAND Corporation, DB-246-OSD, 1999.

Bowie, Christopher J., *The Anti-Access Threat and Theater Air Bases,* Washington, D.C.: Center for Strategic and Budgetary Assessments, 2002.

Bueno de Mesquita, *Principles of International Politics,* Washington, D.C.: Congressional Quarterly Press, 2000.

Byman, Daniel, Peter Chalk, Bruce Hoffman, William Grey Rosenau, and David Brannan, *Trends in Outside Support for Insurgent Movements,* Santa Monica, Calif.: RAND Corporation, MR-1405-OTI, 2001.

Churchill, Winston S., *The Second World War, Volume 1, The Gathering Storm,* New York: Houghton Mifflin Company, 1948.

Clark, General Wesley, *Waging Modern War: Bosnia, Kosovo, and Future Combat,* New York: Public Affairs, May 2001.

Coté, Owen R., Jr., *Assuring Access and Projecting Power: The Navy in the New Security Environment,* Cambridge, Mass.: MIT Security Studies Program, 2000.

Davis, Paul K., Jimmie McEver, and Barry Wilson, *Measuring Interdiction Capabilities in the Presence of Anti-Access Strategies: Exploratory Analysis to*

Inform Adaptive Strategy for the Persian Gulf, Santa Monica, Calif. RAND Corporation, MR-1471-AF, 2002.

Department of Defense, *The Security Situation in the Taiwan Strait* (Report to Congress Pursuant to the FY99 Appropriations Bill, February 1, 1999).

_____, *Quadrennial Defense Review Report*, Washington, D.C., September 30, 2001.

Department of the Army, Headquarters, *Movement Control*, Army Field Manual (FM) 55-10, February 9, 1999, Chapter One.

Gareev, M. A., *If War Comes Tomorrow? The Contours of Future Armed Conflict*, London: Frank Cass & Co, 1998.

George, Alexander L., and William E. Simons, *The Limits of Coercive Diplomacy*, second edition, Boulder, Colo.: Westview Press, 1994.

George, Alexander L., and Richard Smoke, *Deterrence in American Foreign Policy*, New York: Columbia University Press, 1974.

Glenn, Russell, Sid W. Atkinson, Michael P. Barbero, Frederick J. Gellert, Scott Gerwehr, Steven L. Hartman, Jamison Jo Medby, Andrew W. O'Donnell, David Owen, and Suzanne Pieklik, *Ready for Armageddon: Proceedings of the 2001 RAND Arroyo-Joint ACTD-CETO-USMC Non-lethal and Urban Operations Program Urban Operations Conference*, Santa Monica, Calif.: RAND Corporation, CF-179-A, 2002.

Hura, Myron, Gary McLeod, Eric V. Larson, Jim Schneider, Daniel R. Gonzales, D. Norton, Jody A. Jacobs, Kevin O'Connell, William Little, Richard Mesic, and Lewis Jamison, *Interoperability: A Continuing Challenge in Coalition Air Operations*, Santa Monica, Calif.: RAND Corporation, MR-1235-AF, 2000.

International Institute for Strategic Studies (IISS), *The Military Balance 2001–2002*, London: Oxford University Press, 2001.

Jane's Air-Launched Weapons, Issues 27–38, Coulsdon, UK: Jane's Information Group, 1997–2001.

Jane's All the World's Aircraft: 2001–2002, edited by Paul Jackson, Coulsdon, UK: Jane's Information Group, 2001.

Jane's Land-Based Air Defence 2001–2002, Coulsdon, UK: Jane's Information Group, 2001.

Jane's Sentinel Security Assessment—The Gulf States—08, posted January 22, 2001, printed March 22, 2002, from http://www4.janes.com/search97cgi/s97_sgi?action=View&VdkVgwKey=/content1/janesda.

Jane's Strategic Weapons Systems, Issues 35–36, Coulsdon, UK: Jane's Information Group, 2001.

Jane's Underwater Warfare Systems 2002–2003—Submarine and Submersible Designs, posted 14 August 2001, printed January 16, 2002, from http://www4.janes.com/search97cgi/s97_cgi?action=View&VdkVgwKey=/content1/janes.

Jane's World Air Forces 14 [Inventory, Iraq], posted June 21, 2001, printed March 27, 2002, from http://www4.janes.com/search97cgi/s97_cgi?action=View&VdkVgwKey=/content1/janes.

Jane's World Armies 08 [World Armies, Iran—Equipment in Service], January 17, 2000, printed March 22, 2002, from http://www4.janes.com/search97cgi/s97_cgi?action=View&VdkVgwKey=/content1/janesda.

Jane's World Armies 11 [World Armies, Iraq—Equipment in Service], January 2002, printed March 22, 2002, from http://www4.janes.com/search97cgi/s97_cgi?action=View&VdkVgwKey=/content1/janesda.

Kan, Shirley, and Robert Shuey, *China: Ballistic and Cruise Missiles,* Washington, D.C., Congressional Research Service, CRS Report, 1998.

Karasik, Theodore, *Toxic Warfare,* Santa Monica, Calif.: RAND Corporation, MR-1572-AF, 2002.

Khalilzad, Zalmay, and Ian O. Lesser, eds., *Sources of Conflict in the 21st Century: Regional Futures and U.S. Strategy,* Santa Monica, Calif.: RAND Corporation, MR-897-AF, 1998.

Killingsworth, Paul, Lionel Galway, Eiichi Kamiya, Brian Nichiporuk, Timothy L. Ramey, Robert S. Tripp, and James C. Wendt, *Flexbasing: Achieving Global Presence for Expeditionary Aerospace Forces*, Santa Monica, Calif.: RAND Corporation, MR-1113-AF, 2000.

Larson, Eric V., *Casualties and Consensus: The Historical Role of Casualties in Domestic Support for U.S. Military Operations*, Santa Monica, Calif.: RAND Corporation, MR-726-RC, 1996.

_____, "Putting Theory to Work: Diagnosing U.S. Public Opinion on the U.S. Intervention in Bosnia," in Miroslav Nincic and Joseph Lepgold, eds., *Being Useful: Policy Relevance and International Relations Theory*, Ann Arbor, Mich.: University of Michigan Press, 2000, pp. 174–233.

Larson Eric V., and Glenn A. Kent, *A New Methodology for Assessing Multi-layer Missile Defense Options*, Santa Monica, Calif.: RAND Corporation, MR-390-AF, 1994.

Larson, Eric V., David T. Orletsky, and Kristin Leuschner, *Defense Planning in a Decade of Change*, Santa Monica, Calif.: RAND Corporation, MR-1387-AF, 2001.

Majchrzak, Zbigniew, *Army Force Projection*, Fort Eustis, Va.: U.S. Army Transportation School, Deployment Process Modernization Office, 1999.

National Defense Panel, *Transforming Defense: National Security in the 21st Century*, Washington, D.C., December 1997.

National Intelligence Council (NIC), *The Global Infectious Disease Threat and Its Implications for the United States*, Washington, D.C., NIE 99-17D, January 2000.

_____, *Global Trends 2015: A Dialogue About the Future With Nongovernmental Experts*, Washington, D.C., NIC 2000-02, December 2000.

O'Malley, William D., *Evaluating Possible Airfield Deployment Options: Middle East Contingencies*, Santa Monica, Calif.: RAND Corporation, MR-1353-AF, 2001.

Paret, Peter, *Makers of Modern Strategy: From Machiavelli to the Nuclear Age*, Oxford, UK: Clarendon Press, 1990.

Rabasa, Angel, and Peter Chalk, *Colombian Labyrinth: The Synergy of Drugs and Insurgency and Its Implications for Regional Stability*, Santa Monica, Calif.: RAND Corporation, MR-1339-AF, 2001, Chapters Three and Four.

Sergounin, Alexander, *Bordering Russia: Theory and Prospects for Europe's Baltic Rim*, Burlington, Vt.: Ashgate Publishing Company, 1998.

Shlapak, David A., David T. Orletsky, and Barry Wilson, *Dire Strait?: Military Aspects of the China-Taiwan Confrontation and Options for U.S. Policy*, Santa Monica, Calif.: RAND Corporation, MR-1217-SRF, 2000.

Shlapak, David A., John Stillion, Olga Oliker, and Tanya Charlick-Paley, *A Global Access Strategy for the U.S. Air Force*, Santa Monica, Calif.: RAND Corporation, MR-1216-AF, 2002.

Shuey, Robert, "Nuclear, Biological, and Chemical Weapons and Missiles: The Current Situation and Trends," *CRS Report for Congress*, RL30699, August 10, 2001, pp. 1–30.

Stillion, John, and David T. Orletsky, *Airbase Vulnerability to Conventional Cruise-Missile and Ballistic-Missile Attacks: Technology, Scenarios, and the U.S. Air Force Responses*, Santa Monica, Calif.: RAND Corporation, MR-1028-AF, 1999.

Stokes, Mark A., *China's Strategic Modernization: Implications for the United States*, Strategic Studies Institute, U.S. Army War College, 1999.

Swaine, Michael A., and James C. Mulvenon, *Taiwan's Foreign and Defense Policies: Features and Determinants*, Santa Monica, Calif.: RAND Corporation, MR-1383-SRF, 2001.

Swaine, Michael A., and Ashley J. Tellis, *Interpreting China's Grand Strategy: Past, Present, and Future*, Santa Monica, Calif.: RAND Corporation, MR-1121-AF, 2000.

Teal Group Corporation, *International Defense Briefing*, February 2001.

_____, *World Military & Civil Aircraft Briefing [World Military Aircraft Inventory]*, August 2001.

Vick, Alan, *Snakes in the Eagle's Nest: A History of Ground Attacks on Air Bases*, Santa Monica, Calif.: RAND Corporation, MR-553-AF, 1995.

Worldwide Threat to U.S. Navy and Marine Forces, 1995–2015, Defense Intelligence Agency, 2001.

Articles and Papers

Allen, Major Kenneth W., USAF, "People's Republic of China, People's Liberation Army Air Force," Washington, D.C.: Defense Intelligence Agency, DIC-1300-445-91, May 1991.

Arbatov, Alexei G., "The Transformation of Russian Military Doctrine: Lessons Learned from Kosovo and Chechnya," The Marshall Center Papers, No. 2, 2000.

Badkhen, Anna, "Hard-Line Russians Resent Pact with U.S.," *San Francisco Chronicle*, May 10, 2002, p. A13.

Baev, Pavel K., "Russia's Military—The Best Case: Putin's Russia—Scenarios for 2005," *Jane's Special Reports*, February 12, 2001.

Bailey, Kathleen C., "Iraq's Asymmetric Threat to the United States and U.S. Allies," *Comparative Strategy*, Vol. 21, 2002, pp. 161–177.

Barber, Arthur H., III, and Delwyn L. Gilmore, "Maritime Access: Do Defenders Hold All the Cards?" *Defense Horizons*, Washington, D.C.: Center for National Security Policy, National Defense University, October 2001.

Betz, David, "No Place for a Civilian: Russian Defence Management from Yeltsin to Putin," unpublished draft, presented at ISA Conference, Los Angeles, March 15, 2000.

Blank, Stephen, "Should NATO Invite the Baltic States?" *Perspective*, Vol. 12, No. 3, January–February 2002.

_____, "The Return of Nuclear War," *Strategic Studies Institute*, U.S. Army War College, Carlisle Barracks, Pa., January 2000.

Blasko, Dennis J., "Evaluating Chinese Military Procurement from Russia," *JFQ Forum*, Autumn/Winter 1997–1998, pp. 91–96.

Bleek, Phillipp C., "Moscow Reportedly Moves Tactical Nuclear Arms to Baltics," *Arms Control Today*, Vol. 31, No. 1, January/February 2001, pp. 20–22.

Bowden, Mark, *Black Hawk Down: A Story of Modern Warfare*, New York: Signet Books, 1999.

Brooke, Michael, "Vietnam's Geo-Strategic Consideration," *Asian Defense Journal*, November 2001, pp. 4–6.

Cable News Network, "FBI Warns of Shoulder-fired Missiles Threat," reported by Jamie McIntyre, May 30, 2002.

_____, "Missile Downed Russian Helicopter," August 30, 2002.

Chang, Yihong, "China Advances FC-1 Development," *Jane's Defence Weekly*, July 4, 2001, p. 5.

_____, "China Reveals Details of Cross-Country Vehicle," *Jane's Defence Weekly*, February 20, 2002, p. 14.

Clark, Philip S., "EORSAT Launch Ends Year of Low Russian Activity," *Jane's Defence Weekly*, January 9, 2002, p. 11.

Cohen, Ariel, "Russia Deploys Nukes in the Baltics," *United Press International*, Washington, January 4, 2001.

Colton, James D., Paul R. Gefken, David C. Erlich, Steven W. Kirkpatrick, and Richard W. Klopp, "Further Development of Load-Damage Relationships for Chemical Submunitions: Technical Report May 20, 1993–December 1997," DoD Defense Threat Reduction Agency, September 2000, pp. 1–172.

Cordesman, Anthony H., "The Conventional Military Balance in the Gulf in 2000," *Center for Strategic and International Studies*, January 2000.

_____, "Defending America: Redefining the Conceptual Borders of Homeland Defense," *Center for Strategic and International Studies*, January 21, 2001.

_____, "Weapons of Mass Destruction and Asia," *Center for Strategic and International Studies*, February 2001.

_____, "Weapons of Mass Destruction and China," *Center for Strategic and International Studies*, February 2001.

_____, "Weapons of Mass Destruction and North Korea: A Quantitative and Arms Control Analysis," *Center for Strategic and International Studies*, February 2001.

_____, "The Economic and Demographic Challenges to Saudi Stability," *Center for Strategic and International Studies*, May 2001.

_____, "Saudi Military Forces Enter the 21st Century: IX. The Saudi National Guard," *Center for Strategic and International Studies*, August 1, 2001.

_____, "Iraq: A Dynamic Net Assessment," *Center for Strategic and International Studies*, June 16, 2002.

_____, "If We Fight Iraq: Iraq and Its Weapons of Mass Destruction," *Center for Strategic and International Studies*, June 17, 2002.

Covault, Craig, "Chinese Plan Aggressive Satellite Development," *Aviation Week & Space Technology*, November 12, 2001, pp. 56–57.

_____, "China Seeks ISS Role, Accelerates Space Program," *Aviation Week & Space Technology*, November 12, 2001, pp. 52–55.

_____, "Naval Space Ops Crucial to Afghan War," *Aviation Week & Space Technology*, April 8, 2002, pp. 86–87.

Demarest, LTC Geoffrey B., U.S. Army (Ret.), "In Colombia—A Terrorist Sanctuary?" *Military Review*, March–April 2002, pp. 48–57.

Department of Defense (DoD), "Special DoD News Briefing on Defense Transformation," June 12, 2001.

Dokuchayev, Anatoly, "Kaliningrad Talks in Moscow," *Deutsche Presse-Agentur/International News*, February 15, 2001, p. 1.

Donnelly, John M., "Iran Could Have Nukes by 2005: Israeli MOD," *Defense Week*, February 11, 2002, p. 2.

Eavis, Paul, "The Hidden Security Threat: Transnational Organized Criminal Activity," *RUSI Journal*, December 2001, pp. 45–50.

Eftis Trejo, Ceasar J., "Constitutive-Microdamage Modeling of Target-Missile Damage Caused by Hypervelocity Impact: Report for October 1, 1997–August 31, 2000," Texas University at El Paso, Fast Center for Structural Integrity of Aerospace Systems, August 2000.

"Finland Refines Its Future Navy," *Jane's Navy International*, December 2001, pp. 22–29.

Fisher, Richard D., Jr., "China Improves Its Air Force," *China Brief*, Vol. 1, Issue 11, December 10, 2001.

FitzGerald, Mary C., "Russian Military and International Objectives: Interim Strategies and Plans for Long-Term Systemic Change," The Johns Hopkins School of Advanced International Studies, October 29, 2001, pp. 1–33.

Fulghum, David A., "Counterstealth Tackles U.S. Aerial Dominance," *Aviation Weekly & Space Technology*, February 5, 2001, pp. 55–56.

_____, "Global Hawk Crashes in UAE After Afghanistan Mission," *Aviation Week & Space Technology*, January 7, 2002, pp. 24–25.

_____, "Directed-Energy Weapons to Arm Unmanned Craft," *Aviation Week & Space Technology*, February 25, 2002, pp. 28–29.

Gannon, John C., Remarks of National Intelligence Council Chairman at the Hoover Institution Conference on Biological and Chemical Weapons, November 16, 1998.

Garbassen, Gregor, "The Kaliningrad Enclave—Home of Baltic Gold and Rich German Past," *Deutsche Presse-Agentur*, October 2000, pp. 2–5.

Gunaratna, Rohan, "The Asymmetric Threat from Maritime Terrorism," *Jane's Navy International*, October 2001, pp. 24–29.

Hasik, James, "Air Defenses After Kosovo," *Proceedings*, December 2001, pp. 74–77.

Hewish, Mark, "Miniature Underwater Sensors Unveil the Littoral's Secrets," *Jane's International Defense Review*, February 2002, pp. 55–61.

Hodge, Nathan, "U.S. Looks to Extend Homeland Security to Foreign Ports," *Defense Week*, Vol. 23, No. 8, February 19, 2002, pp. 1, 13.

Hooton, Ted, "The Tanker War in the Gulf, 1984–88," *Jane's Intelligence Review*, May 1992.

Hudson, Walter, Commander, U.S. Navy, "SAM Threat Over Iraq," *Proceedings*, October 2001, pp. 32–36.

"Information Challenges to National and International Security," PIR Center, Moscow, Russia, Fall 2001.

Iritani, Evelyn, "Iraq Fights Back with Commerce," *Los Angeles Times*, November 11, 2002.

Jacoby, Radm L. E., U.S. Navy, "Statement of Radm L. E. Jacoby, U.S. Navy, Director of Naval Intelligence Before the Senate Armed Services Committee Seapower Subcommittee on Submarine Warfare in the 21st Century," April 13, 1999.

Karasik, Theodore, and George Allen, *Grozny and Beyond: Health Service Implications of Urban Warfare*, RAND Corporation, AB-540-OSD, February 2002.

Katsva, Maria, "Russia Looks to Expand Nuclear Weapons Option," *ECAAR NewsNetwork*, Vol. 11, No. 1, June–July 1999, pp. 4–5.

Kipp, Jacob, "Russia's Northwest Strategic Direction," *Military Review*, Fort Leavenworth, Kansas, July–August 1999, p. 7.

Knudsen, Olav F., "Soviet Legacy and Baltic Security: The Case of Kaliningrad," as cited on pp. 36–41 in Jakub M. Godzimirski, *Stability and Security in the Baltic Sea Region,* London: Newbury House, 1999.

Kobber, Stanley, "NATO Expansion Flashpoint Number 3: Kaliningrad," Cato Foreign Policy Briefing, February 11, 1998, p. 9.

Komarov, Alexey, "Arms Sales to China, India Bolster Russian Industry," *Aviation Week & Space Technology*, February 5, 2001, pp. 51–52.

"Kosovo i kontrol' nad vooruzhennymi silami," *Voyennyy Vestnik,* No. 5, Moscow: Mezhregional'nyy Fond Infomatsionnykh Tekhnologii, 1999, pp. 1–34.

Kramer, Mark, "NATO, the Baltic States, and Russia," Center for Strategic and International Studies, Working Paper Series No. 19, February 2002, pp. 1–20.

Kusin, Vladimir, "Notes on Kaliningrad," The Potomac Foundation— Special Adviser for Central & Eastern European Affairs, CND/1048, November 9, 1992.

Lee, Wei-Chin, "Thunder in the Air: Taiwan and Theater Missile Defense," *The Nonproliferation Review,* Fall-Winter 2001, pp. 107–122.

Lee, William T., "Putin's Radars Aren't Rusty," *Wall Street Journal,* August 28, 2001.

Levshin, Major General V. I., Colonel A. V. Nedelin, and Colonel M. E. Sosnovskiy, "On Employing Nuclear Weapons to De-Escalate Military Operations," *Military Thought,* Vol. 8, No. 3, 1999, pp. 40–45.

Li, He, "The Role of Think Tanks in Chinese Foreign Policy," *Problems of Post-Communism,* Vol. 49, No. 2, March/April 2002, pp. 33–43.

Lichtblau, Eric, "CIA Warns of Chinese Plans for Cyber Attacks on U.S.," *Los Angeles Times,* April 25, 2002, pp. A1, A19.

Liulevicius, Vejas Gabriel, "Is Kaliningrad Really Lithuania Minor?" Working Paper Series in International Studies, Palo Alto, Calif.: The Hoover Institution, Stanford University, 1996.

McDermott, Jeremy, "FARC Gives Notice of an Urban Campaign," *Jane's Intelligence Review,* September 2002, pp. 24–25.

Minnick, Wendell, "Taiwan Cancels Patriot Contract," *Jane's Defence Weekly,* December 5, 2001, p. 14.

Moshes, Arkady, "Russia's Belarus Dilemma," Council on Foreign Relations, Policy Memo Series No. 182, December 2000, pp. 1–3.

"Navy Shift Elevates Space," *Aviation Week & Space Technology,* April 8, 2002, p. 88.

Novichkov, Nikolai, "Russia Plans to Export Non-Lethal Beam Weapon," *Jane's Defence Weekly,* November 14, 2001, pp. 18–19.

_____, "China Buys Two More Project 956EM Ships," *Jane's Defence Weekly*, January 9, 2002, p. 4.

_____, "Russian Air Forces Facing Protracted Crisis," *Jane's Defence Weekly*, January 23, 2002, p. 4.

_____, "Russia Adopts 10-Year Arms Plan," *Jane's Defence Weekly*, February 6, 2002, p. 16.

Oldberg, Ingmar, "The Emergence of Regional Identity in the Kaliningrad Oblast," *Cooperation and Conflict*, Vol. 35, No. 3, 2000, p. 275.

Patrick, Neil, "Weapons of Mass Destruction: The Threat to the Gulf," *RUSI Journal*, October 2001, pp. 50–55.

Perry, Charles, Michael Sweeney, and Andrew Winner, "Strategic Dynamics in the Nordic-Baltic Region: Implications for U.S. Policy," Dulles, Va: Institute for Foreign Policy Analysis and Brassy's Int., 2000, p. 72.

Perry, Tony, "Fear and Loathing in Kuwait," *Los Angeles Times*, September 30, 2002, p. A1.

Petersen, Phillip A., "Russia's Place in the 21st Century?" The Potomac Foundation, presented at the Conference "Future of Russian Federalism: Political and Ethnic Factors," February 25–26, 2000.

Petersen, Phillip A., and Shane C. Petersen, "The Security Implications of and Alternative Futures for the Kaliningrad Region," The Potomac Foundation, September 9, 1992.

"PLA Exercises Use Missiles in Anti-Carrier Role," *Jane's Missiles & Rockets*, October 2001, p. 4.

Roberts, John, "Checking the Gauge: Western Assessments of Gulf Oil Development," *RUSI Journal*, October 2001, pp. 39–45.

Rubenson, David, and Anna Slomovic, "The Impact of Missile Proliferation on U.S. Power Projection Capabilities," Santa Monica, Calif.: RAND Corporation, N-2985-A/OSD, 1990.

Russell, Richard L., "What If . . . 'China Attacks Taiwan!'" *Parameters, U.S. Army War College Quarterly*, Autumn 2001, pp. 76–91.

"Russia Tests Export Version of Iskander Missile System," *ITAR-TASS*, Moscow, Russia, October 3, 2001.

"Russian Army to Adopt Newest Tactical Missile System in December," *Russian and CIS Arms and Aerospace Market*, Issue 252/26/02, July 2000.

"Russian Fighter Pilots Miss Out on Training Level Increases," *Aviation Week & Space Technology*, February 5, 2001, p. 52.

Sae-Liu, Robert, "PLAAF Fixed-Wing Fleet Cut in Major Restructuring," *Jane's Defence Weekly*, June 14, 2000, p. 41.

_____, "Russia to Make Up China's 'Flanker' Fighter Shortfall," *Jane's Defence Weekly*, June 14, 2000, p. 41.

_____"China Looks to Invest More in Undersea Rescue," *Jane's Defence Weekly*, September 19, 2001, pp. 20–21.

_____, "PLAAF Develops New Airbases," *Jane's Defence Weekly*, September 26, 2001, p. 12.

Schaffer, M. B., "Basic Measures for Comparing the Effectiveness of Conventional Weapons," Santa Monica, Calif.: RAND Corporation, RM-4647-PR, January 1966.

Scott, Richard, "Russia Launches Corvette Programme," *Jane's Defence Weekly*, January 9, 2002, p. 9.

Sengupta, Prasun K., "More Military Hardware Flows into South, Southeast Asia," *Asian Defense Journal*, November 2001, pp. 11–12.

_____, "Robots to Counter Sea Mines," *Asian Defense Journal*, November 2001, pp. 22–23.

_____, "Tactical Airlifters for Ground Combat Forces," *Asian Defense Journal*, November 2001, pp. 24–25.

_____, "PGMs Revolutionize Strike Warfare," *Asian Defense Journal*, December 2001, pp. 22–25.

Shah, Syed Adnan Ali, "Russo-India Military-Technical Cooperation," *Strategic Studies*, Vol. 21, No. 4, Winter 2001, pp. 46–86.

Shuey, Robert, "Nuclear, Biological, and Chemical Weapons and Missiles: The Current Situation and Trends," *CRS Report for Congress*, RL30699, August 10, 2001, pp. 1–30.

Stanton, Colonel Martin N., U.S. Army, "Kamikazes, Q-Ships & Carrier Defense," *Proceedings*, December 2001, pp. 54–57.

Storey, Ian, "Scramble for Cam Ranh Bay as Russia Prepares to Withdraw," *Jane's Intelligence Review*, December 2001, pp. 34–37.

Sulaiman, Sadia, "US Policy in Oil-Rich Caspian Basin," *Strategic Studies*, Vol. 21, No. 4, Winter 2001, pp. 87–115.

Thomas, Lieutenant Colonel Timothy T., U.S. Army (Ret.), "China's Electronic Strategies," *Military Review*, May–June 2001, pp. 47–54.

_____, "Deciphering Asymmetry's Word Game," *Military Review*, July–August 2001, pp. 32–37.

Thompson, Colonel David J., USAF, and Lieutenant Colonel William R. Morris, USAF, "China in Space: Civilian and Military Developments," Air War College, Maxwell Paper No. 24, August 2001.

Tikhonov, Valentin, "Raketno-yadernyi kompleks Rossii: Mobil-nost-kadrov i Bezopasnost," Carnegie Moscow Center, No. 1, 2000.

"Transnational Crime and Its Evolving Links to Terrorism and Instability," *Jane's Intelligence Review*, November 2001, pp. 22–24.

Trendle, Giles, "Cyberwars: The Coming Arab E-Jihad," *The Middle East*, April 2002, pp. 5–8.

Turbiville, Graham H., Jr., "Prototypes for Targeting America: A Soviet Assessment," *Military Review*, January–February 2002, pp. 3–10.

U.S. Joint Forces Command, "A Concept for Rapid Decisive Operations," *Joint Experimentation—J9 Joint Futures Lab*, RDO Whitepaper Version 2.0, October 25, 2001.

_____, "Strategic Deployment," *Joint Experimentation—J9 Concepts Division (J-92)*, White Paper Version 1.0, May 10, 2000, pp. 1–71.

"U.S. Navy to Test Advanced Lightweight Torpedoes," *Jane's International Defence Review*, January 2002, p. 11.

Vick, Alan, David Orletsky, Bruce Pirnie, and Seth Jones, "The Interim Brigade Combat Team: Rethinking Strategic Responsiveness and Assessing Deployment Options," Santa Monica, Calif.: RAND Corporation, forthcoming.

Wallender, Celeste A., "Report of the December 8, 2000 PONORS Policy Meeting," Council on Foreign Relations, February 2001, pp. 1–8.

_____, "The Multiple Dimensions of Russian Threat Assessment," Council on Foreign Relations, Policy Memo Series No. 199, April 2001, pp. 1–2.

_____, "Security Cooperation, Russia, and NATO," Center for Strategic and International Studies, Policy Memo No. 207, November 2001, pp. 1–4.

Wiseman, Paul, "Southeast Asia Islamic Radicals Concern U.S.," *USA Today*, October 30, 2001, p. 10.

"Worldwide Threat to U.S. Navy and Marine Forces, 1995–2015," Defense Intelligence Agency, 2001.

Yunker, Major Chris, USMC (Ret.), "MCM Upgrades Help Solve Riddle of Access Denial," *Proceedings*, September 2001, pp. 68–70.

Zimmerman, Lieutenant Commander John D., USN, "Net-Centric Is About Choices," *Proceedings*, January 2002, pp. 38–41.

Zulkarnen, Isaak, "Main Battle Tank Developments in the Asia-Pacific," *Asian Defense Journal*, November 2001, pp. 18–21.

Web Sources

"9K331 Tor, SA-15 GAUNTLET, SA-N-9, HQ-17," FAS, available at http://www.fas.org/man/dod-101/sys/missile/row/sa-15.html, accessed March 2, 2002.

"America's Air Force Vision 2020," Air Force—Global Vigilance Reach & Power, available at http://www.af.mil/vision, accessed May 4, 2002.

"Annual Report on the Military Power of China," Pentagon, available at http://www.newsmax.com/articles/?a=2000/8/7/160447, accessed December 6, 2001.

"Annual Report to Congress on the Safety and Security of Russian Nuclear Facilities and Military Forces," National Intelligence Council, February 2002, available at http://www.cia.gov/nic/pubs/other_products/icarussiansecurirt.html, accessed February 22, 2002.

"China Analysis: The China-Taiwan Military Balance—Parts 3 and 4," *Asia Times,* January 27, 2000, available at http://www.atimes.com/china/BA27Ad03.html, accessed January 3, 2002.

"China: Missile Programs—Ballistic Missile Summary," Safe Foundation, available at http://www.safefoundation.org/moreinfo/china_missile.html, accessed December 13, 2001.

"Chinese Ballistic Missiles," Center for Nonproliferation Studies, available at http://www.cns.miis.edu/cns/projects/eanp/pubs/chinanuc/bmsl.htm, accessed December 13, 2001.

"Chinese Mines," Jane's, March 6, 2001, available at http://www4. janes.com/search97cgi/s97_cgi?action=View&VdkVgwKey=content1/ janes, accessed January 16, 2002.

"DIA (Defense Intelligence Agency) Testimony to Select Committee on Intelligence: Worldwide Threat to US National Security Interests," available at http://www.securitymanagement.com/library/000255.html, accessed February 22, 2002.

"Documents Enhancing Russia-Belarus Union's Defense Capacity Inked," Pravda.RU, available at http://english.pravda.ru/cis/2001/11/29/22454. html, accessed February 22, 2002.

Falichev, Oleg, "General-Polkovnik Valeriy Manilov: Novaya voyennaya doktrina-adekvatnyy otvet na vyzov vremeni," Krasnaya Zvezda, October 8, 1999, available at http://news.eastview.com.cgi-bin/Sfgate.tr4.

Fisher, Richard D., Jr., "China Increases Its Missile Forces While Opposing U.S. Missile Defense," The Heritage Foundation, available at http://www.heritage.org/library/background/bg1268.html, accessed December 31, 2001.

"Foreign Ground Forces Exercise and Training Assessment (EXTRA): China—January to December 2000," prepared by Mark Coyle, National Ground Intelligence Center, NGIC-1126-0232-02, available at http:// www.ngic.army.smil.mil/products/EXTRA/NGIC-1126-0232-02/0232. html, accessed February 21, 2002.

"Foreign Missile Developments and the Ballistic Missile Threat Through 2015," Central Intelligence Agency, available at http://www.cia.gov/ nic/pubs/other_products/Unclassifiedballisticmissilefinal.html, accessed January 10, 2002.

Gibbons, Jim, "F-22X: The Key to Negating Anti-Access Threats," Electronic Warfare Working Group, Issue Brief #3, March 13, 2001, available at http://www.house.gov/pitts/initiatives/ew/031301ew-brief-3. html, accessed October 8, 2001.

Hackett, James, "China's Military Training Sends Very Clear Signals," Taiwan Studies, available at http://www.taiwanstudies.org/view_story. php3?472, accessed January 3, 2002.

Hsu, Brian, "Navy Allows a Rare Glimpse of Sub," June 23, 2002, available at http://www.dutchsubmarines.com/specials/special_glimpse_seatiger. html.

"Iran Missiles: Overview Chart," Federation of American Scientists, available at http://www.fas.org/nuke/guide/iran/missile/, accessed December 6, 2001.

Isby, David C., "PLA Develops Low-Cost Training for TBM Units," Jane's, available at http://www4.janes.com/emeta/Denial?url=/search97cgi/s97_cgi?action=View&VdkVgwKey=/content1/janes&denial_reason=none, accessed December 6, 2001.

_____, "PLA May be Deploying Rail-Mobile ICBM," Jane's Missiles & Rockets, available at http://www4.janes.com/emeta/Denial?url=/search97cgi/s97_cgi?action=View&VdkVgwKey=%2Fcontent1%2&denial_reason=none, accessed December 6, 2001.

"Iskander/SS-26," Federation of American Scientists, available at http://www.fas.org/nuke/guide/russia/theater/ss-26.html, accessed May 2, 2002.

"Joint Vision 2010," Joint Chiefs of Staff, available at http://www.dtic.mil/jv2010/jv2010.pdf, accessed May 4, 2002.

"Joint Vision 2020," Joint Chiefs of Staff, available at http://www.dtic.mil/jv2020/, accessed May 4, 2002.

Krepinevich, Andrew, "Emerging Threats, Revolutionary Capabilities and Military Transformation," CSBA, March 5, 1999, available at http://www.csbaonline.org/4Publications/Archive/T.19990305.Emerging_Threats,_/T.19990305, accessed October 9, 2001.

Kreydin, Lieutenant Colonel S. V., "Set of Nuc Deterrence Principles, Criteria," FBIS, FTS19990818000125.

Markushin, Vadim, "Neobkhodimost' v takom dokumente davno nazrela," Krasnaya Zvezda, November 29, 1999, available at http://news.eastview.com.cgi-bin/Sfgate.tr4.

Marsh, Nicholas, "Grey Paper 52: Chinese Development of her Military Capabilities," UK Defense Forum, 1998, available at http://www.ukdf.org.uk/gr52.html, accessed January 23, 2002.

Mengxiong, Chang, "Part Four: The Revolution in Military Affairs—Weapons of the 21st Century," Institute for National Strategic Studies, available at http://www.ndu.edu/ndu/inss/books/chinview/chinapt4.html, accessed November 14, 2001.

Moore, Frank W., "China's Military Capabilities," Institute for Defense and Disarmament Studies, available at http://www.comw.org/cmp/fulltext/iddschina.html, accessed January 3, 2002.

Moscow Strana.ru National Information Service, "Chief of Missile and Artillery Troops Interviewed on New Weapon Systems, High-Precision Weapons," November 19, 2001, FBIS, CEP20011119000180.

Myers, Gene, "Getting to the Fight: Aerospace Forces and Anti-access Strategies," March 27, 2001, available at http://www.airpower.maxwell.af.mil/airchronicles/cc/myers01.html, accessed October 8, 2001.

"Nations/Alliances/Geographic Regions: Eurasian Republics—Russia," Periscope, updated November 1, 2000, printed 3/22/02 from http://www.periscope.ucg.com/nations/eurasia/russia/airforce/index.html.

"Nations/Alliances/Geographic Regions: Middle East/North Africa—Iraq," Periscope, updated September 1, 2001, printed 3/22/02 from http://www.periscope.ucg.com/nations/mideast/iraq/airforce/index.html.

"Natural Resources Defense Council—Nuclear Notebook: Chinese Nuclear Forces,1999," Bulletin of the Atomic Scientists, Vol. 55, No. 4, May/June 1999, available at http://www.bullatomsci.org/issues/nukenotes/mj99nukenote.html, accessed December 31, 2001.

"Northeast Asia: Goal and Interests," available at http://www.defenselink.mil/pubs/prolif97/ne_asia.html, accessed December 13, 2001, pp. 1–13.

"Obsuzhdaem Proekt Voyennoy Doktriny. Prioritety Voyennogo Stroitel'stva," Krasnaya Zvezda, October 13, 1999, available at http://news.eastview.com.cgi-bin/Sfgate.tr4.

"Overview: PLA Navy Facilities," Federation of American Scientists, available at http://www.fas.org/man/dod-101/sys/ship/row/plan/index.html, accessed December 28, 2001.

"Putin Denies Nuclear Weapons Move," available at http://www.cnn.com/2001/WORLD/europe/01/06/russia.germany/index.html.

Rashchepkin, Konstantin, "Commander Shpak Summarizes Airborne Troops' Training Year," December 3, 2001, FBIS CEP2001120300-0360.

Shepard, Stacey, "Preparing for the Anti-Access Threat: Looking Beyond the 2MTW Posture," CSBA, September 27, 2000, available at http://

www.csbaonline.org/4Publications/Archive/P.20000927.Preparing_For_ The_/.

_____, "RMA and the Future of Land Forces: Era of Tank Primacy is Over," CSBA, April 20, 1999, available at http://www.csbaonline.org/ 4Publications/Archive/P.19990420.RMA_and_the_Future, accessed October 8, 2001.

Sidyakin, Anatoliy, "Obsuzhdaem proekt voyennoy doktriny. V takom dele nel'zya speshit," Krasnaya Zvezda, November 19, 1999, available at http://news.eastview.com.cgi-bin/Sfgate.tr4.

"Submarines and Submersible Designs," Jane's Special Reports, August 14, 2001, available at http://www4.janes.com/search97cgi/s97_cgi?action= View&VdkVgwKey=/content1/janes, accessed January 16, 2002.

"Submarines—Attack Submarines (SSN) China, People's Republic: HAN Class (Type 091)," Jane's, May 23, 2001, available at http://www4. janes.com/search97cgi/s97_cgi?action=View&VdkVgwKey=/content1/ja nes, accessed January 16, 2002.

"Submarines—Strategic Missile Submarines, China, People's Republic: XIA Class (Type 092)," Jane's, May 23, 2001, available at http://www4. janes.com/search97cgi/s97_cgi?action=View&VdkVgwKey=/content1/ janes, accessed January 16, 2002.

"The Geostrategic Environment and Its Implications for Land Forces—The Land Forces: The Versatile Force," Army Vision 2010, available at http://www.army.mil/2010/geostrategic_environment.html, accessed October 29, 2001.

Tirpak, John A., "Bomber Questions," Air Force Magazine, Vol. 84, No. 9, September 2001, available at http://www.afa.org/magazine/Sept2001/ 0901bomber.html, accessed October 8, 2001.

"Unclassified Report to Congress on the Acquisition of Technology Relating to Weapons of Mass Destruction and Advanced Conventional Munitions, 1 July Through 31 December 2000," Central Intelligence Agency, available at http://www.cia.gov/publications/bian/bian_sep_2001.html, accessed September 18, 2001, pp. 1–12.

"Underwater Weapons—Unclassified Projects, China, People's Republic," Jane's Air Launched Weapons, March 6, 2001, available at http://www4. janes.com/search97cgi/s97_cgi?action=View&VdkVgwKey=/content1/ja nes, accessed January 16, 2002.

"US DoD Reports China's Growing Missile Power," Jane's Missiles & Rockets, August 1, 2000, available at http://www4.janes.com/contnet/janesdata/mags/jmr/history/jmr2000/jmr0028/.htm, accessed December 6, 2001, pp. 1–4.

Walpole, Robert D., "The Iranian Ballistic Missile and WMD Threat to the United States Through 2015," Statement for the Record to the International Security, Proliferation, and Federal Services Subcommittee of the Senate Governmental Affairs Committee, September 21, 2000, available at http://www.odci.gov/cia/public_affairs/speeches/archives/2000/walpole_missile_092200.html, accessed December 6, 2001.

Warrick, Joby, "Iraqi Drones May be Used to Spread Death," *Washington Post*, September 6, 2002, available at http://www.washingtonpost.com.

"ZRK-SD Kub 3M9: SA-6 Gainful," Federation of American Scientists, available at http://www.fas.org/man/dod-101/sys/missile/row/sa-6.html, accessed March 2, 2002.